John M. Oesterreicher

GOD AT AUSCHWITZ?

Foreword by Michael Wyschogrod
Afterword by Thomas R. Peterson, O.P.

Institute of Judaeo-Christian Studies
Seton Hall University

CONTENTS

FOREWORD

IT MAY WELL be that a time will come when the Holocaust, the murder of six million Jewish men, women and children by the Nazis, will no longer be a difficult theological problem. This may come about in one of two ways. We may, in time, simply forget what happened in Treblinka and Babi Yar, and then the Holocaust will no longer trouble us. Or, God forbid, our future in this atomic age may hold such horrors in store that in comparison with them the Holocaust will pale into insignificance. It is difficult to say which of these two ways of forgetting the Holocaust would be more terrible.

As of now, decent Jews and Christians have not forgotten the Holocaust. And because they have not forgotten it, they are struggling with a difficult question: How can we, after the Holocaust, remain believing Jews and Christians? Does it still make sense to speak of a loving God in light of the fact that God remained silent at Auschwitz and did not save the suffering victims? Is it not time for Jewish and Christian theology to draw the consequences of this silence and conclude that the God of Israel died in the murder factories of the Third Reich?

There are, indeed, those who would draw this conclusion. They tell us that after Auschwitz, we cannot carry on our theological business as usual, that to do so is to mock the victims, that the old formulas are hollow and obscene in the presence of their suffering. They speak of human history now being divided into the pre- and post-Holocaust era, and nothing in the "post" era is similar to anything in the "pre" era. What they do not tell us is how one lives in the post-Holocaust era, how one retains the possibility of love, and why we do not all become Nazis in a world in which the God of Israel no longer lives.

Msgr. Oesterreicher's reflections on the Holocaust are the reflections of a man who, under the infamous Nuremberg

1

Laws, would have been included in the ranks of the victims, had he not been able to flee in time. He is aware of "what some of my loved ones had been through, and what I had been spared...." He thus stands at a unique vantage point from which, as a convinced Christian, he probes the martyrdom of the Jewish people, a people from whom the Nazi Moloch permitted no exit.

Msgr. Oesterreicher's faith is not destroyed by Hitler. He does not, of course, have an "explanation" of why God permitted that which happened to happen. But he does know one thing. God shared the suffering of the victims. He was not high up in heaven, looking down at the turmoil, taking note of the chimneys

> When Israel's body drifted as smoke
> Through the air.... (p. 20)

God suffers alongside his people Israel. He joins them in their exile, feels their pain and will rejoice at their redemption. This is an authentic rabbinic idea, however objectionable it may be to Jewish Aristotelianism of later times.

It would, of course, be understandable if Jews were made uncomfortable by this idea. Does a God who suffers alongside, even on behalf of man not point in the direction of Jesus? Does Msgr. Oesterreicher hint at a connection between the suffering of Jesus and that of the Jewish people? He says that "out of respect for Jewish sensibilities" he has not pursued this direction (p. 45). But the direction is there.

For many Jews, such a Christological interpretation of Jewish suffering is objectionable. They see it as the intrusion of Christian categories into the deepest pain of Israel, not altogether different from the offensive teaching, nowhere to be found in Msgr. Oesterreicher's essay, that Jewish suffering is the righteous punishment inflicted by God for Israel's rejection of its redeemer.

While this latter teaching is, indeed, objectionable, the opinion that Israel is especially beloved of God and "the Lord

2

reproves whom he loves" (Proverbs 3:12) is Jewish. And so is the teaching that the prophet and the Jewish people suffer for the sins of others (Isaiah 53 remains part of the Hebrew Bible). It is essential that authentically Jewish beliefs not be denied simply in order to widen the division between Judaism and Christianity.

Wherever the Holocaust deprives Jews or Christians of their faith in a redeeming God, the Holocaust continues to claim more victims. And when the reality of the Holocaust serves to put an end to the teaching of contempt of Judaism by Christianity, Hitler is further defeated and the memory of his victims sanctified. It is for this reason that Msgr. Oesterreicher's essay deserves careful attention.

MICHAEL WYSCHOGROD

INTRODUCTION

THIS ESSAY ON the rabbinic vision of God's fidelity to His people in time of great suffering is a fruit of my lasting concern with the great problem posed by the Holocaust. It was written in the late seventies. It is of small moment why it was not published then, but it is witness to God's providence that it can be done so now.

The late Miss Suzanne Jobert, benefactress of the Institute of Judaeo-Christian Studies from its birth, bequeathed it funds that were to serve the various concerns of the Institute. Her generous gift coincides with a renewed onslaught by certain corrupters of history, seeking to deny the reality of Hitler's mass murder of Jews.

Recently, a "Committee for Open Debate on the Holocaust" bought advertising space in college and university newspapers, asserting that the story of the Holocaust was a hoax, that there was never a plan or order by Hitler to annihilate all Jews within the reach of Nazi power.

It is true that there exists no written order by Hitler — not because he was a gentle soul who never touched a single hair on anyone's head, but because he was a mixture of bravado and cowardice. Like all dictators, he wanted to appear a noble man. He did not leave behind a written command to slaughter Jews and others whom he considered enemies, but he gave oral orders for doing away with them.

In his book, *Hitler und die Endloesung* "Hitler and the Final Solution" (Munich: Limmes, 1982) Gerald Fleming describes an interview of 1922 between Dr. Josef Hell, a German journalist and later a major in the army of the Reich, and Adolf Hitler who had not yet achieved, but lusted for, power. Among the questions Hell posed was how Hitler would deal with the Jews once he had full freedom of action. No sooner had Hell posed this question than Hitler gazed

4

into empty space. In a paroxysm of hate he raged that, on the largest square of Munich, he would have a series of gallows erected — as many as traffic allowed — and hang Jews on them "till they stink!" He would continue doing this till the last Jew in Munich was eliminated, and do exactly the same in other cities till all of Germany was rid of Jews (p. 27f).

Though Hitler never carried out this fiendish scheme, his resolve of ending Jewish presence in Europe remained unchanged. Braggart that he was, he told the Czechoslovakian Minister of Foreign Affairs, Frantisek Chvalkovsky, that to avenge the death of Ernst von Rath, third secretary of the German Embassy in Paris, at the hand of Herschel Grynszpan, a young Jew despondent about the merciless deportation of his parents from the Reich: "We will annihilate the Jews in Germany" (p. 39). Similarly, in 1941 he pledged to the Grand Mufti of Jerusalem, Haj Amin Husseini, an unrelenting war against the Jews (p. 116).

Two years earlier, as he started World War II by attacking Poland, he fabricated his own alibi. In addressing the Reichstag in January 1938, he avowed: "If the international Jewish financiers... should succeed in plunging the nations once more into a world war, then the result will be... the annihilation of the Jewish race in Europe!" (William Shirer: *The Rise and Fall of the Third Reich* (New York: Simon and Schuster, 1960) (p. 964.)

To divert attention from his grandiose plan of bringing all of Europe and more under his sway, he portrayed the Jews as the secret rulers of the world and the source of all evil. In *Mein Kampf*, they were said to spread syphilis in order to contaminate Nordic blood and to manage worldwide prostitution. They established democracy, the cause of political chaos. They even invented — oh, horror! — conscience, he once told Hermann Rauschning, a Danzig official. (*The Voice of Destruction* (New York: Putman, 1940) (p. 223-224.) As the people of the Decalogue, they were a constant irritant, even an obstacle. He viewed them as the hinderers of a plan to have the so-called Nordic race conquer and rule most of

5

Europe and lands beyond. Therefore, they had to disappear from the face of the earth.

The Nazis sought ever more efficient means of ridding Germany of Jews because their first measure, forced emigration, had been stopped by the onset of war. The second measure, that of mass-shooting of Jews in the "East" by SS commandos had not achieved its goal quickly enough. Though this fact is rarely mentioned, certain SS officers felt ill at ease with their "mission." First Heydrich, then Himmler, Reichsfuehrers of the SS, silenced critics by saying that the killing of Jews was the Fuehrer's order, and as such had the force of law; it had to be carried out with unquestioned obedience (Fleming, p. 63-68).

Because mass shooting was not efficient enough, gas chambers were built. The pseudo-historians who deny the reality of the Holocaust, stating that "there was no order, no plan, no budget, no weapon," have a small point in saying that there was no weapon, because Zyklon B gas is not one, in the normal sense of the word. At the risk of belaboring the issue, I will state again that there was no written order. Hitler never signed a decree that Jews had to be sent to the gas chambers. Loudmouth though he was, he shunned reality. During the war, he never went near the battle line; even his command post was set up at a very safe distance from it. His directives were given orally; strangely, he vacillated between wanting and not wanting to be identified with the mass slaughter of Jews.

Only hours before his suicide, however, according to William Shirer, Hitler implicitly admitted his lead in the annihilation of Jews. In his "Political Last Will and Testament," he demanded the continuation of his war against them, and threatened them with an undying hatred by all those who would remember that they, and they alone, bear "responsibility... for the millions of deaths suffered in the battlefield and in the bombed cities." Hitler, the master of the Big Lie, went further still, declaring the Jews guilty of their own massacre (Shirer, p. 1124). Though devoid of all power, he continued his game: "Above all, I enjoin the

6

Government and the people to uphold the racial laws to the limit, and to resist methodically the poisoner of all nations, international Jewry" (p. 1126).

It is quite common for an assassin to deny his guilt in court, but it is rather rare for writers and committees to whitewash a mass murderer who considered his orgy of hate a contribution to the general welfare. In sum, to declare the various death camps with their systematic program of annihilation of Jews — not to speak here of other victims — a figment of Jewish imagination, and to do this in the face of the minutes of the infamous Wannsee Conference, the witness of many American liberators — officers and soldiers — photos, eye-witness accounts, particularly that of the commandant of Auschwitz — above all, the untold pain suffered and countless tears shed by the survivors — is the height of temerity.

Still, I dare to say with Mephistopheles that those twisters of history are "part of that power that plots evil, yet works good." (Goethe, *Faust*, Part I). Since we humans tend to repress all that is troublesome, those "twisters" serve a good purpose in reawakening our conscience. I am grateful that they have stirred me to rush into print a manuscript set aside for too long.

When first I worked on this study, I felt very much alone in seeking to make known the rabbis' vision. I would be an ingrate were I not to acknowledge that there were others who, without knowing it, strengthened me in my resolve.

I am happy to end my introduction with words of thanks to two friends who prefaced and concluded this study. Michael Wyschogrod, Ph.D., a noted Jewish thinker, Visiting Professor of Religion at Houston University, formerly Professor of Philosophy at Baruch College, C.U.N.Y., makes me his debtor for confirming my reading of the Rabbinic lore regarding Israel's anguish. I am no less beholden to the gracious Chancellor of this University, Father Thomas Peterson, O.P., a disciple of St. Thomas Aquinas and student of Far Eastern thought, for his praise of my work which I fear I may not

7

fully deserve. I am particularly grateful to him for showing that the Rabbinic vision of God's presence in the midst of earthly hells ought to be applied to today's many sufferers.

For the last two years, my eyesight has deteriorated. I would like to express my gratitude to Mrs. Dolores Cunningham for helping me with the final version and Sr. Sofie Mueller for her tireless work in giving the manuscript its shape. Father Lawrence Frizzell, Associate Director of the Institute of Judaeo-Christian Studies was kind enough to read the proofs.

Last but not least, I thank those of my readers who are daring enough to enter a world of thought hitherto unknown to them.

JOHN M. OESTERREICHER

A Note on the Rabbinic Sources of this Study

THE RABBINIC SOURCES from which I have drawn answers to the question posed by the title of this study are twofold: the Talmud and Midrashic literature.

Those unfamiliar with the Talmud may assume it to be a book. Yet, it is not a single tome but a series of tomes, a library. In the well-known English translation, the Soncino edition, it comprises 35 volumes. The Talmud ("Teaching") has been transmitted in two versions: The Palestinian Talmud (*Talmud Yerushalmi*) and the Babylonian Talmud (*Talmud Babli*). It has been estimated that the original text of the latter consists of two and half million words.

The contents of two Talmudim are the result of discussions held in the Palestinian and Babylonian Academies, institutions for the study of the Written and the Oral Torah. The Written Torah is the "Five Books of Moses," while the Oral Torah contains interpretations of the laws and statutes of the former. Orthodox Judaism holds that the Oral Torah was given to Moses at Sinai along with the Written Torah.

The two versions of the Talmud, thus, record, in the main, the teaching and legal opinions of rabbis over a period of eight centuries. Some scholars will trace the very beginnings of the Talmudic traditions to the Babylonian Exile, or at least to the time of Ezra (see Neh 8:6-9).

For quite some time, the explanations and interpretations of the Law were not organized and, thus, were often confusing. Sages of the second and thirds centuries A.D. brought the various traditions into a system which was finally authorized by R. Judah Ha-Nasi around 200 A.D., or as Jews say C.E. meaning Common Era. The system was called Mishnah ("Teaching").

9

The Mishnah is made up of six orders, *sedarim*: Zeraim ("Seeds") deals with laws on farming; Moed ("Appointed times") lists laws governing the liturgical year; Nashim ("Women") treats, in the main, laws regulating marriage and divorce; Nezikin ("Damages") discusses civil and criminal law; Kodashim ("Holy things") offers regulations about the Temple service; Toharot ("Purity") considers laws upholding ritual purity. These orders are subdivided into tractates varying between seven and twelve in number.

The entire Babylonian Talmud consists of sixty-three tractates. For most talmudic tractates, the Mishnah constitutes the very basis of every chapter; it is followed by extensive comments called Gemara ("Completion").

The legal observations of the Talmud are interspersed with historical, scientific, and medical references, parables, anecdotes, folklore, customs — Jewish and non-Jewish — remarks on demons and magic, and, not least of all, religious and moral admonitions. These non-legal offerings have been estimated to make up one-third of the Babylonian Talmud.

The most comprehensive codification of talmudic laws, even those not applicable outside the land of Israel, or as the rabbis will say, "The Land" is the Mishneh Torah by R. Moses ben Maimon (Maimonides), who lived from 1135-1204.

Though the Talmud serves observant Jews as a religious "textbook," it is no longer the ultimate authority on legal matters. That quality has passed to Codes and *Responsa*. The standard work accepted by Orthodox Jewry is the *Shulhan Arukh* ("The Set Table") by Joseph Karo of the 16th century in Safed, Galilee. Moses Isserles of Poland added notes to Karo's work. It is arranged according to subject matter, rather than following the sequence of the tractates of the Talmud.

Responsa are answers to legal problems by famous rabbis throughout the centuries; more than half a million of the *Responsa* have appeared in print.

Prior to the fall of Jerusalem in 70 A.D., Torah (here understood as the whole of the Hebrew Scriptures) together with the Temple, that is the worship of God through prayer and sacrifice bound various groups and movements into the chosen People of God. (The community of Qumran is an exception to the rule in not having recognized the legitimacy of the Temple service.) After the Temple's destruction, first the Mishnah, much later Mishnah and Gemara — the whole Talmud— became the unifying bond that kept Jewry alive and one.

To the uninitiated, the Talmud is a labyrinth through which it is hard to find one's way. Varying, at times conflicting, opinions do not make its understanding easier. In the past, some Christian writers, in an attempt to widen the rift between the Jewish and the Christian Way, denounced the Talmud as an anti-Christian work. They were wrong. Yet, no less wrong are those Jewish apologists who deny that the Talmud contains no opposition to the Christian message. These dissensions are, I trust, about to disappear. Thus I am happy that I can offer passages from rabbinic literature that can serve the meeting of minds estranged for centuries.

Another, indeed major, source of rabbinic teachings on the Divine response to the catastrophes in Jewish history is midrashic literature. "Midrash" derives from the Hebrew *darash* ("seek," "search," "investigate").

Midrashim are, thus, writings in search of hidden meanings in a biblical line, story, or passage in the more than literal, the fuller sense of Scripture. The rabbis believed every verse, every word, indeed, every letter to be alive with special significance. The interpretations tended to apply the words of Scripture to the need of the people of their time.

Some Midrashim are running commentaries on Scripture, while others are homilies on feasts and special Sabbaths. Midrashim on the Pentateuch and on the "Five Scrolls"

11

(*megillot*), Song of Songs, Ruth, Ecclesiastes (Kohelet), Esther and Lamentations form *Midrash Rabbah* (The Major Midrash); I draw on it time and again. Other Midrashim I have relied on are *Pesikta de Rav Kahana* and *Pesikta Rabbati*. Pesikta ("section") is so called because the work deals with chosen passages. Still another Midrash I refer to is the *Mekhilta*, ("measure") which, is primarily a halakhic (legal) commentary on the latter part of Exodus. It gives the rules by which laws are to be deduced. Thus, both are collections of homilies for festivals, or outstanding Sabbaths. The Midrash on the Psalms, (*Midrash Tehillim*) is a mine of inspiration.

All through rabbinic literature the study of Torah is exhorted and exalted so much so that one is apt to think that the study of Torah is all that counts. Yet, Rabbi Simeon ben Gamaliel (1st cent. A.D.) says that the doing of the Word, the carrying out of God's law, is one's uppermost duty (*Av*. I,17).

THE HOLOCAUST POSES grave questions. Indeed, its very existence seems a question offering no answers. Why was there an Auschwitz and other branches of hell? Are there enough words adequate to express the horror of the savagery Hitler unleashed on the Jewish people? Jews were worked to death in salt mines. They were machine-gunned so that they would fall into pits they themselves had dug; most were dead, but some were still alive as other victims tumbled over them. When the executioners found these and other methods not efficient enough, they had their victims first choked to death, and then burned to ashes beyond recognition. For Hitler and his henchmen, the extermination of Jews had to be complete, "final," without bodily trace.

I

AN UNANSWERABLE QUESTION

THERE ARE NO words to describe the evil that devised the "Final Solution," or the agonies its realization caused. This is not to say that I subscribe to the pseudo-existential view of the human condition as one of questions, questions only, never of answers. Nor do I agree with the occasional suggestion that no answer to this hellish enterprise should ever be tried, that our question must remain open like a running sore. In one of his books, Elie Wiesel, great wrestler with the problem of the Holocaust, has lifted this stance to a high plane. Turning to the Lord, he prays: "I no longer ask You to resolve my questions, only to receive them and make them part of you."[1] In these pages, I go counter to this attitude. Rather do I ask God to grant me some insight, and I do not do so lightly.

Many years ago, when first I heard the reports of the Nazi death camps and caught a glimpse of that world of terror, and fathomed the pain of the victims, I retreated into myself. Realizing what some of my loved ones had suffered,

13

and what I had been spared, I withdrew into total silence. My anguish seemed a matter between God and me, not to be shared with others. Before an ocean of evil, talk seemed empty, powerless, serving no good purpose.

Years later, when circumstances prompted me to speak out, I continued to skirt the question that had been and still is on many lips, on the lips of those who walk in the sight of God, as well as on the lips of those who give His presence not a moment's thought: Where was the Holy One of Israel when, in a *danse macabre* across all Europe, hatred led Jews to an early and cruel death? I do not wish to avoid my responsibility. In spite of those who use the question as a subterfuge to escape the total surrender faith and love demand, I must answer it. For it has severely tried many Jews and Christians, shaken them to the core, even robbed them of their faith.

But, I am not so arrogant as to seek an original answer, even were it possible to do so. In solving the riddles of human existence, originality more often than not is a curse. Rather than search for novel answers, I would like to examine the Jewish tradition for its response.

Some of my friends have wondered why I, a man who has entrusted his life to Christ, would not rather develop a Christian theology of pain and death. I will return to this question toward the end of this essay. For the moment, it will suffice to recall that most victims of Nazi atrocity were Jews. Those beset with questions and doubts today are, for the most part, Jews. I know a few who, in the privacy of their hearts or the intimacy of a face-to-face conversation, ask devastating questions.

Is the God of Israel the ever-present God who spoke from the burning bush (Ex 3:14) or is He, as some maintain, an absent God? Is He the Almighty whom we profess in our prayers, or is He often powerless — no more than a creative force that does not, that cannot care? Has He perhaps two faces — one benevolent, the other malevolent? Questions like these agitate many. Jews, even those living thousands of miles away from the sites of the crematoria, or born years after those ovens were extinguished, experience themselves as victims; Christians, in a spirit of solidarity, wish to share their pain. Is it not imperative, therefore, that the answer to these questions spring from Jewish sources, the wisdom and compassion of the rabbis who tried to face earlier catastrophes?

In the course of its history, Israel has suffered and — let us never forget — survived near fatal disasters, the most grievous among them the Fall of Jerusalem under Titus in 70 A.D. "The angels of peace" are said to have "wept" over the destruction of the Temple (bHag. 5b). Even more expressive of its cataclysmic nature is the rabbinic view that God Himself roars like a lion at each of the three watches of the night: "Woe to the children, on account of whose sins I destroyed my house and burnt my Temple and exiled them among the nations" (bBer. 3a).

The ruin of the Temple and the razing of Jerusalem lead to questions like these: How did the mourners over Zion view such a disaster? How did the rabbis comfort their people in the anguish of exile? How did they reconcile Israel's sin and suffering with the Lord's goodness and power? And, what does their vision of YHVH as the God of Humility and Self-abandonment, of Pity and Pain — that is, as the One who feels for His own and shares in their suffering — tell Jews and Christians of this day? Can it, perhaps, quiet the nagging question whether or not human existence is meaningful? Can it give sudden light to those among us who think that they are like people walking through a dense forest whose trees and branches do not let the sun break through?

II
THE UNIQUENESS OF THE HOLOCAUST

ALL WHO SEEK to relive the Holocaust in the depth of their being are at one in the view that it is unique in the known history of humanity. The evil that begot Hitler's death factories as well as the factories themselves are without parallel.

In a very real sense, every sufferer feels his or her pain as something incomparable. My headache, not to speak of my inner sorrow, is unlike the one endured by another person. In speaking of a person, I think of a human being in the concreteness and singularity of his or her existence, open to the world and to its maker, free and responsible for his or her acts.[2] For all that a given human being has in common with all other human beings, he or she is unique. Each lives but once; no life can ever be repeated. Similarly, every human event — happy or painful — is without parallel.

It goes without saying that I do not wish to analyze an individual victim's encounter with the death the Nazis prepared for Jews. As a deeply personal experience, it is largely closed to me; in fact, I would not wish to invade that sanctuary of pain. The Holocaust's objective singularity, however, demands my attention.

BEYOND MEASURE

It is not the frightening number of murdered Jews — six million — that makes the Holocaust unparalleled in its manifestation of evil.[3] Stalin killed more than six million Kulaks because they resisted his plan for the socialization of all farmlands. Mao sent more than six million Chinese to their death in order to remove all those who could have impeded his revolution. No, the uniqueness of the Holocaust does not lie in its number of victims, however astronomical. Its measure is beyond measure.

To degrade any individual or group is ultimately to assault the Creator; to attack Jews is consciously or more often subconsciously, to plot against Christ. As reported by the Jewish chronicler Ephraim bar Jacob, Bernard of Clairvaux so castigated the twelfth-century riff-raff that had joined the Second Crusade for easy spoils. Marching down the Rhineland, they slaughtered the Jews in the cities on the way. In no uncertain terms, the Saint told them that one who lays hands on a Jew is as much a sinner as one who lays hand on Jesus Himself.[4] All this is true of the Holocaust as well; in fact, it is true to so eminent a degree that the Nazi persecution and murder of Jews is a phenomenon *sui generis*, to all who know its gravity, an evil without equal.

CAMOUFLAGE

Nazi propaganda offered a number of reasons for the exclusion of Jews from German society — the prelude to their "banishment" from the earth. Here are some alleged reasons: The great number of Jewish physicians, bound to poison Aryan blood, were ruining the health of the State. The disproportionate number of Jewish lawyers, bent on destroying Germanic law, with its sense of honor and nobility of the strong, were a constant danger to the German people. Jewish publishers and journalists, writers and poets, artists and musicians, actors and entertainers exercised a pernicious influence on the lives of all.

"A Jew who writes in German lies" was one of the slogans of those days. Another maintained that Jews dedicated to intellectual endeavors were *Kulturbolschewiken*, Communists determined to subvert all the provinces of culture to their own accursed end. Finally, the real or supposed power of Jews in trade, industry, and finance was declared disastrous. There were, after all, two types of capital, "Aryan" and Jewish, *schaffendes und raffendes Kapital*. The "Aryan" capitalist was said to be "creative," producing goods for the well-being of the *Volksgemeinschaft*, while the Jewish capitalist was considered an exploiter, "grabbing and stealing" from others, mindful only of his own wealth.

The charge that Jewish physicians plotted the poisoning of "Aryan" blood is preposterous. The notion that Aryan tycoons were angels while Jewish manufacturers were devils is equally absurd as are all the other allegations. Normally, they would not have impressed many, but their constant repetition brainwashed uncritical minds.

THE WAR AGAINST GOD

Even if one assumes for a moment that the allegations were true , it is not clear why the "criminals" alone were not executed, rather than an entire people. Does not the wholesale murder of Jews prove that the rationale was an elaborate sham, meant to camouflage the true motive? That motive was Hitler's rancor against the theological quality inherent in the Jewish people, the invisible "power" of the community who stood at Sinai. Instinctively, Hitler felt that the Jewish people who received the gift of the Law and, no less the Church who brought the Commandments to the nations, were obstacles on the road to Nazism's absolute power. Paradoxically, these two communities, devoid of arms or significant political power, stood in the way of the firm establishment of a society governed by the principle "might makes right."

Hitler once called conscience "a Jewish invention [that] mutilates Man." On the same occasion, he declared: "There is no such thing as truth... One must distrust mind and conscience, one must place one's trust in one's instinct."[5] As long as Jews and Christians were alive, their very existence was an irritant and a reproach. Their mere presence spoiled his dream of becoming mas-

18

ter of the earth, so strong was their representative, symbolic character. Hitler's *ressentiment* was nourished by megalomanic jealousy. "There cannot be two Chosen Peoples. *We* are God's people," he told an interlocutor while banging on a table. If there was a chosen one, he felt, it had to be himself and that bigger self, the German people.[6]

The ideological mantle of Hitler's revolt was woven by several writers and thinkers. Nietzsche, for instance, wrote: "Christianity, sprung from Jewish roots,... is the anti-Aryan religion par excellence. [It] is the transposition of all Aryan values, the victory of chandala values (those common to the Untouchables.)[7] Or: "The poor man's god, the sinner's god" went with the chosen people into strange lands. Though he won half the earth to his side, "he has remained a Jew, he has remained the god of back streets,... of dark holes, of shacks, of all the unhealthy quarters of the world! His universal kingdom is, now as always, a domain of the underworld, a hospital, a basement realm, a ghetto kingdom."[8] Nietzsche and other forerunners of Hitler had not the foresight to realize how inflammatory their ideas were. All that was needed was an arsonist like Hitler to burn the flesh of Jews to ashes. (Ashes, it cannot be stressed enough, seem the very antithesis of life: cold and gray, they spell "nothingness.")

In the past, Jews were persecuted for what seemed like religious reasons, yet were often but reasons of money and power. In our time, the Nazi persecutors of the Jews spoke of economy, politics, race; in reality, they waged a religious war, the religious war to crown them all. They battled God, Christ, election, grace, and mercy. In 1949, the American-born French writer Julian Green mused:

> Jesus' torment goes on in this world, day and night. Having once been nailed to a Roman cross, He has been persecuted with inexorable cruelty in the person of His own people. One cannot strike a Jew without having the same blow fall on Him who is the Man par excellence and, at the same time, the Flower of Israel. It is

19

Jesus who was struck in the concentration camps. It is always He, His suffering is never ended.[9]

MAN, MACHINE AND DEHUMANIZATION

One of the singular features of the Nazi mass murder is the complicity of Man and Machine. In the death camps, modern technology — meant to enrich our lives and ease our burdens — was turned into a foe of life. For the first time in human history, cruelty became a conveyor belt for the elimination of men, women, and children. In Auschwitz, mass murder became so efficient that on a given day, ten to twenty thousand corpses could "roll off" the assembly line of hate.

Unprecedented, too, is the calculated dehumanization process that took place before the actual murder. At all times, cruel rulers and violent mobs have sought to kill, lusting for blood. The Nazis, however, did not wish to see blood, what they craved was the degradation of their victims. Jews had first to be robbed of their dignity and individuality: the victims had to line up, naked, one after the other, till they became one huge mass of flesh. Thus they were divested of their initiative and power to resist: classical music accompanied them to gas chambers disguised as "washrooms" in order to lull their fears or suspicions. Only then did their "overseers" let the poisonous gas pellets do their deadly work.

It was not the passing whim or the individual aberration of some camp commander that deprived Jews of their humanity; systematic dehumanization was the inevitable result of the Nazi ideology which declared that Jews were vermin. In a document, published by the headquarters of the SS, called *Der Untermensch*, the Jew is said to be the eternal enemy of Man, nature's ill-fated shot at making a human being, a mere counterfeit. The Jew is said to be ruled by a "chaos of wild, unrestrained passions, by a

20

boundless drive toward destruction, a primitive greed, and an undisguised meanness — the subhuman being."[10]

Never before has hatred of others been so clearly unmasked as a mirror, or rather disguise, of self-hatred. When we become angry at others, we react to a real or imagined injury inflicted on us. More often than not, we are also annoyed at our own faults as we see them reflected in the souls of our adversaries. All Jew-baiting exemplifies this psychological mechanism. But no other form of abusing Jews has reached such "perfection" as Nazism: The Jews as *Untermensch*, as "sub-human being," is nothing but the product of a gigantic cover-up. Consciously or subconsciously, the Nazis projected their own evil impulses and wicked schemes onto Jews.

WITHOUT HOPE

In the course of history, people have been threatened because of their possessions or actions; their convictions, ideas, or faith; their real or alleged crimes. As a rule, people have been persecuted because of a feature of their lives they were responsible for. Yet, in their plight, they were not without escape: They could avoid "punishment" by regretting their actions, relinquishing their possessions, recanting their ideas, rejecting their convictions, or abandoning their faith; in short, they could escape by a change of mind, orientation, or life. No such evasion, and thus no hope, was open to Hitler's Jewish victims. It did not matter whether their minds, lives, virtues, faith, or loves were exemplary or not; "blood" sealed their fate. The wise and the fools, the rich and the poor, the committed and the uncommitted, saints and sinners, all fared alike. Has there ever been a world in which nothing carried weight except the dubious notion of race? It was the time of total eclipse of the human spirit.

WITHOUT FRIENDS

All who passed through Hitler's murder centers sensed that
they were doomed; they felt abandoned in their agony.
They suffered without anyone to comfort them, anyone to
stay the murderous arms of their jailers; they died without
friends at their side. In the eyes of the victims, the churches
and academies of learning; democratic as well as totalitarian
regimes; parties of the left, and the center; the West and the
East — all seemed deaf to their cries of agony.

Some may counter that the spectacle of indifference, or
rather the scandal of silence, was not confined to the suffering of the Jews at the hands of the Nazis. To list only a few
instances: The world took no notice of the mass slaying of
Armenians by the Ottoman Empire in 1915. No one worried
about the lot of the Tibetans when in 1950 their country was
invaded and annexed by Communist China. In the sixties,
the whole world heard of African tribes fighting, even massa-
cring each other, but no one intervened. For years, the
Ugandan dictator Idi Amin had killed thousands, possibly
hundreds of thousands of his countrymen; yet, his black
neighbors treated him as if he were an honorable ruler,
indeed, the brother of all blacks.[11] Now and then, the newspapers speak of the "terror of death" in Cambodia, but the
world did nothing to stop the killing. Again, everyone who
endures agonizing pain feels ultimately alone, abandoned,
forsaken.

All this seems to indicate that those who walked that
hellish way to the gas chambers only shared in the loneliness
of any creature-in-pain. But this is not the whole picture.
The Jewish share in human suffering over the centuries
appears to be greater than that of most other peoples but,
more importantly, the persecutions visited now on one
community of Jews, now on another, have sharpened their
susceptibility to pain to an intense degree. This heightened
sensitivity reached its climax in the torments of the Holocaust. In the gas chambers and on the way to them, the
candidates for "extermination" were isolated from their kin;

husbands and wives, parents and children were separated from one another. All other tokens of humanity — compassion, help, warmth, and solace — were withheld. In this, Jews were not only victims of Man's inhumanity toward Man but the prototype of the sufferer forgotten by others and, it often seems, by God as well.

III
CHALLENGING GOD

"THE WHOLE CREATION in all its parts groans as if in travail"
(Rom 8:22). In a rare vision of cosmic dimension, the
Apostle sees suffering at the core of all that has been made,
readying the whole of nature for a share in the glory-to-come,
for a part in the freedom, peace, and joy of God's children.
Ephemeral and perishable, swinging between birth and
death, between growth and decay, this universe anxiously
expects to be renewed. This is also the teaching of some of
the Jewish apocalyptic writings at the time of the Second
Temple — that is, the time between the completion of the
Hebrew Scriptures and the destruction of Jerusalem. (See IV
Ezra 7:55; Syr Apoc Bar 32:6.) Subjected to seeming "futil-
ity," the world sights and throbs with pain, waiting for the
day when God's love will "flood our hearts" (Rom 5:5) and
creation's innermost being as well. But these are sighs and
groans that a human ear cannot hear.

THE CREATURE IN PAIN

As far as I know, wild beasts, too, suffer very much in silence; unless locked in mortal combat, they die, apparently
without uttering much of a sound. Human beings, however,
often cry out in pain. If this observation is correct, could it
be that animals instinctively perceive death as the inevitable
end of the process of organic life while human beings realize
in the depths of their hearts that death contradicts their
personal existence, that it should not be? Am I right in
thinking, that standing at the tomb of Lazarus, Jesus' heart
reveals that death is not the original design of Man's creation? The deuterocanonical Wisdom of Solomon expressly
declares: "God did not make death, nor does He delight
[in it]" (1:13).

24

Human beings, in any case, are driven to tell God and the world of their torments, to look for love, for companionship, for help. There are exceptions to this urge of the human heart. Socrates, for instance, thought that wisdom demanded him to meet death without a creature's anguish, to die without passion, indeed calm and composed. In this, Socrates seems the kind of Greek who longs to be, not a human being in his fullness, but a demigod.

Jesus — truly Jewish in this as in many other ways, and truly human in this as in all His actions — is not ashamed of emotion, indeed of His own humanity. Wrestling for total surrender to His Father's will in the Garden of Olives, He prays in anguish that the cup of suffering may pass (See Lk 22: 42-43). On the cross, He does not hide the travail of His soul; on the contrary, He shouts His desolation into the world for all to hear. He does not call into the emptiness of space but to His Father's heart. He dies in love and in truth: Pain is pain, not an illusion; death, though a door to life and glory, is an anomaly. For all its natural causes, it is more closely related to sin than to creation, more to Man the miser than to God the generous Giver.

TOTAL GRIEF

In the torture camps too, victims pleaded with God as did many survivors, some in deep sadness, others in fierce anger. The questions: "Where was God?" and "Why did He look on the horrors without striking down the torturers?" unite the Holocaust — its uniqueness notwithstanding — to all the torments of Israel, to all human grief. Two poetic voices, that of Nobel Laureate Nelly Sachs and that of Yiddish writer Zvi Kolitz, may speak for many others. Steeped in grief at a world from which goodness and joy seem gone forever, Nelly Sachs let her heart lament in the opening lines of two of her poems:

O the chimneys
On the ingeniously devised habitations of death

When Israel's body drifted as smoke
through the air...[12]

O the night of the weeping children!
O the night of the children branded for death!
Sleep may not enter here.
Terrible nursemaids

Have usurped the place of mothers...
Instead of mother's milk,
panic suckles these little ones...[13]

Her "Eli: A Mystery Play of the Suffering of Israel" takes place in a Polish town, soon after the dread of extermination has ended. A few survivors gather at the marketplace around a fountain. A washer woman relates the story of the eight-year old Eli. One morning, when Eli saw his parents being dragged out of the house and driven to their martyrdom, he ran after them. He had his shepherd's pipe with him. Pointing it to heaven, he piped to God, begging His mercy. A soldier, who saw Eli, mistook his gesture for a secret signal and "struck him down dead with his rifle butt."

Though justice and compassion seem to have departed from this earth, Nelly Sachs is not without hope. She is confident that the rhythm in which her play is written shows something of Hasidic fervor, able to lead actors and audience to an "encounter with the divine radiance which accompanies each of our everyday words." She trusts that this fervor, made manifest in the rhythm of her play, will "raise the unutterable to a transcendental level, so as to make it bearable..."[14]

ANGER AT GOD'S SILENCE

In a story, variously called "From the Burning Ghetto" or "Yossel Rackover speaks to God," Zvi Kolitz lets a Jew from the Polish town of Tarnapol, descendant of a line of Zaddikim, assume the role of a modern Job. We hear him say that in the world-to-come, he will bring down his "clenched fists on the table of the Almighty and demand an explanation" of the trials Israel has had to undergo. "This is what I am going to do as soon as I stand before my angry Creator."[15]

"Formerly, when all was well with us," Yossel Rackover continues, "my feeling toward Him was toward One who had always shown me His grace and in whose debt I stood. Now, however, I feel that He owes me something, too. Now, I think I have the right to admonish Him..." Yossel then offers this clue to the mystery of our age: "Something extraordinary is taking place in the world — ours is the time when the Almighty turns His face away from those who pray to Him."[16]

No matter how disappointed, how angry, Yossel Rackover is chained to God. Thus, he exclaims:

> You say that we have sinned. Of course, we have sinned. That one must be punished for it, I can understand. But I demand that you tell me if there is a sin in the world that merits a punishment as great as this... Perhaps you will say that now there is no question of punishment and expiation, that you have only turned your face away and have abandoned men to their instincts. But I ask of you, O God, and this question consumes me like fire: What more must happen before you will turn your face to us again?[17]

Yosel Rackover concludes his plaint with this confession:

> These are my last words to you, my angry God: You will not succeed. You have done everything to make me lose my faith, to make me despair. Nevertheless, I die as I have lived, my faith in you firm as a rock.

Blessed be forever and ever the God of the dead,
the God of vengeance, the God of truth and of the
Law, who soon again will show His face to the
world and will make its foundations tremble by
the sound of His almighty voice.

Hear, O Israel, the Lord is our God,
the Lord is One![18]

The Lord on Trial

Zvi Kolitz has endowed this witness of his people's murder
by the Nazis with singular passion and rare power of speech.
Christians as much as Jews listening to his indictment of
the Lord cannot help being stirred by the depth of feeling,
particularly if Yossel Rackover's "brief" is read in full.
Christians, however, are likely to counter: "The creature's
relationship to the Creator is never that of plaintiff to defen-
dant." I agree. Still, I will not argue with a man tormented
in the depth of his soul while on the threshold of a cruel
death. There is something sacred about every sufferer. Only
an anxious heart that has not stopped loving will question
God's providence.

One must not ignore the fact that Yossel Rackover,
fictional character though he be, speaks not only for himself
but also for other victims of the death-brokers of Nazi years.
Moreover, he is heir to a powerful tradition of Jews wrestling, even arguing with God.

As a matter of fact, Zvi Kolitz's tale is patterned after an
earlier one, which Solomon Ibn Verga (end of 15th cent.)
incorporated in his father's book *Shevat Yehudah*, "Staff of
Judah" (Judah is the tribe from which Spanish Jewry claimed
to have descended). Yossel Rackover himself refers to the
older story of a Jew who, seeking to escape the Spanish
Inquisition, takes refuge on a ship. While out on the high
seas, lightning kills his wife; a storm tosses his child into the
water. "Alone, without a crumb of comfort, naked, barefoot,

beaten..., terrified," he arrives at a wild desert island. He turns to God, charging Him to "have done everything to destroy my faith." "O my God and God of my fathers," he continues, "You will not succeed... You may take from me all that is dear and precious on earth, You may torment me to death — yet I will always believe in You. I shall always cling to You, in spite of Yourself." Yossel Rackover's defying profession of lasting faith is a reprise of that earlier pledge of loyalty in deepest adversity, even to the point of its conclusion: *Shema Yisra'el*, "Hear, O Israel, the Lord is One."[19]

An extreme, seemingly reckless, stance can be found in the *Pesikta Rabbati*, a ninth-century collection of discourses by Palestinian rabbis of the third and fourth centuries A.D. Though generations had passed since Jerusalem fell in 70 A.D., the destruction of the Temple was still an open wound. Israel in exile needed soothing words, the rabbis felt. Thus one of them, interpreting the beginning of the Second Isaiah's message, "Comfort, comfort my people, says your God" (Is 40:1), told his congregation that as soon as the Holy One, blessed be He, turns to Jerusalem with an offer of comfort, Jerusalem will reply:

> "I will accept no comfort from you till I and you have reproved each other, as is said: 'Come, my Beloved, let us go forth into the field' (Ct 7;12), a place where no business is conducted but ours..." Jerusalem will go on to say: "Master of the universe, why did you not deal with me as Joseph did with his brothers, as is said: 'Oh that you were like a brother to me?' Ct 8:1). Think of Joseph — his brothers requited him with evil and wished to slay him, yet when they came under his power, he requited them with good and himself comforted them, as is said: 'And he comforted them, and spoke kindly to them' (Gn 50:21)." (*Pes. R.* 30,4)[20]

The commentator on Isaiah 40 does not stop here; he goes so far as to predict:

> At once the Holy One, blessed be He, will accept the reproof from Jerusalem, and will say: "I was foolishly arbitrary with you, as is said, 'I acted in a lordly fashion toward you' (Jer 3:14)." Jerusalem will reply: "Master of the universe, is it right that what you are saying be kept only between us? Who will let the nations of the earth know about me that I have done your will? They revile, abuse, and mock me, saying, 'You rebelled against your God and you were faithless to Him.'"

God then promised — the redactor of *Piska* 30[21] tells us — to speak to the nations of the earth and make known Israel's righteousness.

GOD THE SUPREMELY OTHER

That the Holy One of Israel (Is 1:4 passim) should be in the dock strikes a Christian as strange. True, God draws close to Man by affection and friendship, favor and care; still, He is always the supremely Other.

> Who is like You, O Lord, among the mighty;
>   Who is like You, majestic in holiness,
> Awesome in splendor, working wonder!
> (Ex 15:11)

So hails an ancient song attributed to Moses and the Israelites as they extolled God's mighty deeds in rescuing His people. Begging Him to spare Sodom for the sake of the righteous, Abraham declares: "Here I venture to speak to my Lord, I who am but dust and ashes" (Gn 18:27). When Isaiah, seeing God in His glory, was called to be His spokesman, he cried:

> Woe is me! I am lost,
>   for I am a man of unclean lips

and I dwell among a people of unclean lips
yet with these eyes I have seen the King,
the Lord of hosts. (Is 6:5)

These and other confessions by biblical figures show
how, according to its Scriptures, ancient Israel saw Man's
relationship to God. Even more pertinent in our context is
Job's admission. Tried to the utmost, he has argued against
his "friends" who see his suffering as punishment. For
them, divine justice follows the rules of arithmetic; for
them, the life of a human being and God's blessing are like
the two parts of an equation. In defending his innocence,
however, Job has gone too far. When confronted by God
himself:

Will the fault-finder argue with the Almighty?
He who chides God, let him answer for it.
(Job 40:2)

Job answers:

I am nothing: what can I answer you?
I put my finger to my lips. (40:4)

Yet, he is not let off that easily. The Lord demands of him
that he stand up like a man and answer questions, among
them this one:

Dare you deny that I am righteous,
put me in the wrong that you may be right?
(40:8)

There is irony in Job's vain attempt to prove his innocence by declaring God guilty. To shift blame to others or to
"distribute" it among some or many is a device common to
human beings everywhere. To have proclaimed, however,
God's disapproval of such shirking of responsibility is one of
Israel's honors. I am thus inclined to think that the *darshan*,
the "expounder" whom I quoted a moment ago, does not
represent the summit of the Jewish tradition. But, this may

31

be my Christian bias. It seems that the argument with God and the submission to Him are both essential parts of the rabbinic tradition. Or, in the words of the late Rabbi Jakob Petuchowski, "the 'argument with God' is as authentic and as noble a Jewish posture as is the absolute submission to the divine will."[22]

If I, for one, feel ill at ease with the view of the divine-human bond as a kind of contest, or the thought that the relationship between the Lord and His creatures is that of two partners in a fencing match, I do not mean to repeat the old imputation of legalism. It is entirely legitimate to view the Lord's bond to His people in the image of a juridical trial, as long as it does not become the total vision. The prophets, one must not forget, for instance, present God's response to Israel's failures, to its offenses against the covenant, in the form of litigation. Isaiah, for example, has the Lord accuse His sinful people in open court, with heaven and earth as witnesses (Is 1:2-4). The cosmic setting seems necessary because Israel's wrongdoing taints all creation, as does ours. The awesome framework, with God as prosecutor and judge, bespeaks God's majesty and holiness which will not tolerate sin.

Tempting though it must be to answer God's charge with a countercharge, I do not think that the attempt to introduce the adversarial system of our civil and criminal courts into our dealings with God is a happy one. I wonder whether quarrel, argument, or search for fairness ever leads to an increase of love. Yet, appearances notwithstanding, love — it is not for me to say how great a love — seems to have inspired our unnamed preacher to suggest the reproving session. Does he not use a line from the Song of Songs to support His demand: "Come, my Beloved, let us go forth into the field" (see *Pes. R.* 30, 4; page 29 of this study)? R. Jakob Petuchowski, whom I quoted a moment ago, holds out for the *possibility* that the vision of God suffering with His people is "itself an 'answer' to the question raised in the 'argument with God' — an 'answer' which may never have been given if the 'question' had not been raised to begin with."[23]

IV
LOVE'S TRIUMPH

Pᴇsɪᴋᴛᴀ Rᴀʙʙᴀᴛɪ Is a collection of various discourses: not only do the personalities and times of its commentators vary, their visions vary, too. Small wonder that this midrashic anthology contains a corrective of, or answer to, the approach I have just discussed. One of the sermons deals with Israel's steadfastness in the sight of God, and applies Proverbs' praise of the "woman of valor" to the community of Israel. "She does Him good and not evil all the days of her life" (Prov 31:12), the Midrash quotes, and then continues:

> [With Israel's valor before Him], the Holy One, blessed be He, could say to the ministering angels "Come, and I will make known to you the valor of my children. Lo, I have laden them with many afflictions in this world; I brought chastisements on them... in each and every generation, yea, in each and every hour; yet they do not rebel, rather they call themselves wicked.... They speak thus: 'We have sinned. We have done wrong, we have committed outrage, we have transgressed. We have turned away from Your commandments and judgments. Yet, our sinning has done us no good. In all that has come upon us, You have been righteous, for You acted in truth (that is, in fidelity) while we have done wrong!'" (Pes. R. 35)[24]

Here Israel forgets itself and grows in love so that the midrash can apply to the community the words from Proverbs: "A woman of valor who can find?" (31:10)

In this midrash, Israel approaches God on the knees of its heart. Never is Israel as tall as when it bows before Him. (The same, of course, is true of any man or woman.) There

33

are other witnesses to the posture. The great Midrash of the Song of Songs interprets the verse: "I am love-sick" (Ct 2:5) in various ways. The most moving one is this:

> The community of Israel
> said to the Holy One, blessed be He,
> "Master of the universe,
> all the ills you bring on me
> are to make me love you more." (*Cant. r.* II, 5,1)

A talmudic saying breathes the same spirit:

> Raba — some claim, Rav Hisda — said,
> "If someone is visited with chastisements,
> he should search his deeds.
> Has he done so and found no cause,
> he should attribute (his trials) to his
> neglect of Torah.
>
> Once he has attributed them
> to idleness in studying Torah
> and still found nothing,
> he can be sure that they are chastisements of love.
> As it is said in Proverbs 3:12
> 'For the Lord reproves whom He loves'"
> (*bBer.* 5a)

FRUIT OF SUFFERING

Modern Jewish writers insist that Judaism has never extolled suffering for its own sake. Still, R. Simeon b. Yohai can praise it on account of its fruits.

> The Holy One, blessed be He,
> gave Israel three precious gifts,
> All of them He gave only through suffering:
> The Torah, the Land of Israel, and the
> world-to-come. (*Ibid.*)

34

The rabbis even go so far as to admonish their own to rejoice in chastisements rather than in prosperity:

> If a man lives in good fortune all his days,
> his sins are not forgiven.
> How are they forgiven?
> through chastisements. (*Sifre Dt. 32*)

So meaningful do the trials God permits us to undergo appear to the rabbis that the praise of pain can even go to this height:

> Beloved are sufferings.
>   For as sacrifices atone
> so do sufferings...
>   They atone even more than sacrifices
> Sacrifices affect only a person's property,
>   Suffering, however, his whole being.
>   (*Mekh. Bahodesh* 10)

ISRAEL'S PERDURANCE

When the rabbinic sages speak of the nobility of suffering, they do not do so lightly. They are strangers neither to personal nor communal sorrows; they have all been tried. With the rest of the people, they mourn for Zion. Yet, in accepting God's will and judgment, in calling Him righteous, they thus become righteous themselves. And so it is with the people of Israel:

> What did the Holy One, blessed be He,
>   say to them?...
>   "In what contrast to Israel's steadfastness,
>   consider Egypt's want of it.
> I brought only ten plagues upon the Egyptians,
>   but the [ancient] Egyptians are extinct, gone.
>
> Consider the kingdom of Babylon.
>   Upon the Babylonians

I brought only a small measure of troubles
but they could not withstand them,
    thus the Babylonians came to naught
    and are gone from the world....

As for Israel,
    even though I bring trouble and
chastisements
upon them...,
they do not recoil from me,
but remain steadfast.
Therefore they endure forever and ever."

(Pes. R. 35:1)

Need I spell out the bearing of this and the other passages on the spiritual response of Jews and Christians to the Holocaust, and the shape our life should take in its wake?

V
THE GOD OF PITY

To Rise To the fullness of its calling, Israel — and with it every human being — needs to acknowledge its creaturely state and "walk humbly with (its) God" (Mi 6:8). No special intelligence is necessary to understand this dependence; yet, it takes depth to see that humility is also an integral part of God's perfection.[25]   R. Yohanan b. Neppaha, a Palestinian teacher of the third century, observed that whenever Scripture hails God's greatness or might, it hastens to praise His humility, His self-abandonment, too (*bMeg.* 31a).[26] So pervasive is the rabbi's belief in God's humility that amidst several magic formulae for the cure of all kinds of ills there is even one addressed to a thornbush:

> O thorn, O thorn,
>> not because you are taller than all other trees,
> did the Holy One, blessed be He,
>> have His *Shekhinah* rest upon you,
>> rather because you are lower than all other
>> trees...
>
>> *(bShab.* 67a)

The rabbis never tire of saying that God could have revealed Himself from the top of the world's highest mountains, yet He humbled Himself and spoke out of a bush. R. Eleazar b. Arakh (ca 90 A.D.) was so moved by this self-abandonment that he applied to God the proverb: "One lowly in spirit wins honor" (Prov 29:23). He joyfully quotes verse 6 of Psalm 138: "Exalted as He is, the Lord cares for the lowly" (see *Mekh. de R. Simon b. Yohai* on Ex 3:2). As God passed over all those magnificent trees in favor of an unsightly shrub, so He ignored all those majestic mountains and beautiful hills and "came down" (Ex 19:20) on Sinai, a mount in the wilderness, to give Israel the Torah (see *bSot.* 5a).

37

Another favorite theme of the rabbis is this: God "left" the inaccessible height of His glory, His throne above the seventh celestial dome (a mythological symbol of His transcendence, His supermundane existence) in order to be in the midst of His people, in the Dwelling — the Tabernacle — which, according to Exodus 26:7, is covered with "sheets woven of goat's hair" (see *Midr. Tanh.* on Ex 26:7). Again, the Lord who knows no dimensions or measurements, who "fills the heavens and the earth" (Jer 23:24), confines Himself to the smallest place on earth; He even speaks out of the heart of the burning bush[27] (see *Ex.r.* Shemoth).

BEARER OF ISRAEL'S SIN

Still more moving is the observation of R. Eleazar b. Pedat (ca 270 A.D.) that in seven biblical passages, the Holy One, blessed be He, puts Himself on the same footing as the bowed-down and the afflicted (*Mdr. Tanh.* on Is 66:1-2).[28] To attain the fullness of their existence, a man or woman must strive for humility. God need not strive; He *is* humble, the rabbis tell us. In interpreting the verse, "How long shall I bear with this evil generation?" (Nm 14:27), *Midrash Rabbah*, among other sources, tells us that the Holy One, blessed be He, said:

> A man buys a slave
> > so that he may take a lantern
> > and give light to his master
> > as the latter goes from place to place,
> But I, the Master,
> > take a lantern and
> > (on your march through the desert) give you
> > light though you are my servants.
> > > *(Num. r. 16:27)*

So that no one should take the rabbis for mere flatterers of
their people, let me add that this exposition is preceded by
one quite different:

> The Holy One, blessed be He, said:
>   "The nations of the world honor me and
>   show me respect.
> But you, you provoke me.
>   I bear with you, but how long
>   shall I suffer?" (*Ibid.*)

Still another comment on this verse makes use of
Halakhah. Rabbinic law says that a man may carry his son
on the Sabbath, even though the child holds a stone in his
hand, or a basket with a stone inside it. God, too, carried
Israel through the desert — "as a father carries his son" (Dt
1:31) — even though that generation had an idolatrous image
with them (see Jgs 17:3). Israel heaped sin upon sin, but the
Lord forgave, time and again. His faithfulness notwithstanding, He is impelled to ask, "How long must I tolerate this
wicked, murmuring community?" (see *Num. r.* 16:26). To
lesser minds, this divine complaint might spell the end of
God's patience, and of His covenant with Israel. To the
rabbis, it speaks, paradoxically enough, of God's never-
ending patience. According to them, God bears Israel
and its sin.

The rabbis go still further. The Lord not only carries
Israel in its sin and suffering, He suffers too. He suffers
because of them and with them. R. Simeon b. Lakish, a
Palestinian teacher of the third century, is most graphic in
the description of the sorrow Israel caused its Lord:

> The Holy One, blessed be He, said:
>   "It would have been to my honor,
>   had I had no dealings with this people."
> For when Israel had to go into exile among
>   the nations of the world,
>   the Holy One, blessed be He,
>   went round to the doors of the nations
>   to listen to what they were saying.

What did the "eavesdropping" Lord hear? He heard His name profaned, His power belittled, and "He grew old," as it were. Grief "aged" him (see *Lam. r., Poems of the Sages*, 15). He even wept and said:

> Woe is me! What have I done?
>> I caused my *Shekhinah* to dwell on earth
>> for the sake of Israel.

> But now that they have sinned,
>> I have returned to my former habitation...
> And I have become a laughter to the nations,
>> a byword to human beings. (*Ibid.* 24)

The same R. Simeon tells that on three occasions the ministering angels wanted to sing before God, but were denied permission; first, when the Flood covered the earth and destroyed all life; second, when the Egyptians pursuing the Israelites drowned in the Sea; third, when the Temple was destroyed. R. Simeon then puts the prophet's words on the lips of the Holy One, blessed be He, and makes Him say:

> Turn your eyes away from me,
>> let me weep bitterly.
> Do not try to comfort me. (Is 22:4)

Should some readers be scandalized by these apparently demeaning anthropomorphisms, I would like to assure them that the rabbis knew how daring they were. They were fully aware of the incongruity of all statements that speak of God in human terms; at the same time, they realized the need of the human heart to speak of Him, and of the impossibility of doing so, except in words and images that speak to the heart. Hence they like to qualify their anthropomorphic portrayals of the Lord by adding: "If one may say so" or "If this comparison can be made."

The Divine Fellow-Sufferer

As God bears Israel's sin, so He bears its burden. Indeed, He is eager to do so. Psalm 22:9 is frequently rendered: "He relied on the Lord; let (the Lord) deliver him." Matthew's Gospel relates that at Jesus' crucifixion the crowd present taunted Him, and that members of Jerusalem's officialdom joined in the jeering. Unable to understand His voluntary impotence, His non- resistance, they are said to have shouted: "He trusted in the Lord, let the Lord rescue Him" (Mt 27:43). Far be it from me to deny that this was so, or to maintain that Jews, their leaders included, have without fail been compassionate. Through the sufferings they had to endure in the past, Jews have acquired a feeling for the pains of others so that one can indeed speak of compassion as a Jewish trait, but no human heart is totally immune to the temptation of maliciously delighting in another's misfortune or defeat. Gentiles who assume that at Golgotha a typically Jewish attitude was at work are not only wrong, unfair, unkind, they are fools as well — fools because they do not know themselves.

The *Midrash on Psalms* gives a different reading of Psalm 22:9. "Roll (your anguish) on me, and I shall bear it." It justifies this reading by another psalm verse:

> Cast your care upon the Lord,
> and He will support you. (Ps 55:23)

The Midrash continues:

> R. Yohanan told the parable of a king and his son. The son was given a heavy beam to carry. When the father saw this, he said: "Lay upon me every burden you wish, and I will bear it." In a similar way, the Holy One, blessed be He, says to Israel: "Roll the burden of your sins upon me, and I will bear them." (*Midr. Ps.* 22,22)

41

The rabbis go still further in their teaching:

> When Israel's sins brought it about that enemies invaded Jerusalem, the enemies seized Israel's warriors and bound their hands behind their back. Thereupon the Holy One declared: "Scripture says of Me, 'I will be with him in trouble' (Ps 91:15). Since My children are deep in trouble, can I remain at ease?" At once, (because Israel's hands had been bound by their enemies), "God bound His right hand behind His back" — if one dare speak thus — "on account of the enemy" (Lam 2:3). (*Pes. de Rab Kahana*, 17,5)

Later in the same passage, we are told that the Holy One intimated to Daniel in the final vision granted him (see 12:13):

> I have set a term for my right hand's being bound.
>> As long as My children are bound in slavery,
>> My right hand shall be bound with them.
> When I deliver My children,
>> I shall deliver My right hand." (*Ibid.*)

Since God in heaven shares in Israel's suffering, it is impossible for Him to forget His people's anguish, unless He wants to forget His "right hand" and His own pain. Hence: "The delivery of Israel stands thus for the delivery of God, His being freed from His suffering, His chains."[29] Several times, the rabbis return to the divine promise: "I will be with him in his distress." *Midrash Rabbah* interprets this assurance in the spirit of Is 63:9: "In all their afflictions He was afflicted" — this, at least, is the midrashic reading of the verse. Thus the same Midrash has God say to Moses:

> Do you realize that I live in misery
>> just as Israel lives in misery.
> The place from which I speak to you
>> — a thornbush —
> Ought to tell you that I am their partner
>> in misery, as it were." (*Ex. r. 2,5*)

42

The same vision of God as suffering with Israel is expressed more strongly in a comment on these protestations of love in the Song of Songs: "My sister, my love, my undefiled" (5:2). According to *Midrash Rabbah*, it is the Holy One, blessed be He, who addresses Israel by these names. He calls Israel "my sister" because the Israelites were closely knitted to Him by the blood of the Passover and the blood of circumcision. He also calls the people "my undefiled," "my perfect one" (*tamati*). By a change of vowels, a device that rabbis enjoy, this is made to read either *tamuti* or *teumati*. The first word can be rendered "my devoted one" for the people pledged their hearts to God at Sinai when they said: "All that the Lord has said we will do, and obey" (Ex 24:7). The second word means "my twin." God so humbles Himself that He declares Himself not greater than His people; that Israel almost becomes the main figure in the blood relationship that ties God to "her." R. Joshuah of Siknin (4th cent. A.D.) said in the name of R. Levi:

> As with twins,
>> when the head of one aches,
>> the other aches too,
> So the Holy One, blessed be He,
>> feels Israel's pain as it were, saying,
> 'I will be one with him in distress.' (Ps 91:15).

Thus what grieves one, also grieves the other. When Israel hurts, the Holy One, blessed be He, hurts, too (*Pes. R.* 15,6 and *Cant. r.* 5,2,2,).

VI
A THEOLOGY OF THE HEART

I THINK I ought to say once more why I searched the writings of the ancient rabbis, and not Christ's gospel, for an answer to the tormenting question: Where was the God of righteousness when His children suffered unspeakable pain? When a friend of mine, an Anglican priest, learned of my quest, he wrote:

> In reverently thinking about the Holocaust...,
> a Jew, and even more explicitly a Christian, must
> take into consideration the fall of angels and of
> Man...

> According to the New Testament witness,
> Jesus came into the world to redeem Man from
> the consequences of the fall. In line with the Old
> Testament and rabbinic traditions, He accom-
> plished this through vicarious suffering.

> Jesus was a Jew. Christians have attributed
> to Jesus the image of the Suffering Servant. I
> therefore propose that, mysteriously, the cruci-
> fixion of Jesus and the suffering of the Jewish
> people are linked, as every innocent suffering is
> somehow linked to Jesus' crucifixion.

It is out of respect for Jewish sensibilities that I have not pursued the direction suggested by my friend.

Some Jews tend to see in the image of the Suffering Servant a kind of justification of their oppressors and perse-cutors. Though this is hardly sound exegesis, it is an emo-tional reality, and I have to defer to it. The answer I have been looking for is one that could speak to both Jews and Christians. While searching for common ground, I could have developed a theology of freedom: In creating human

44

beings and granting them the freedom to choose good or evil, life or death, the Maker of the world plainly imposed limitations on His omnipotence. Once they were free, they could sin, abuse the precious gift bestowed on them. To cap it all, when human freedom reached its height of expression, evil, too, took on a dimension up to then unheard of. A theology of freedom is momentous because it summons human responsibility to action. Thus, it satisfies the mind. But can it also still the restless heart? I fear not.

MIDRASHIM AS A BRIDGE

Midrashic literature may fulfill this purpose. Its theology is, after all, one of the heart, not of reason: one that moves toward truth, not along the arduous route from premises to conclusion, but intuitively and, in the best sense of the word, emotionally. It is not by chance that the *Pesikta de Rab Kahana* hails the grandeur of the human heart in these words:

> According to Scripture, the heart can see, the heart can hear, the heart can speak, the heart can know, the heart can stand, the heart can fall, the heart can walk, the heart can cry out, the heart can be glad and the heart can be comforted. (see *Piska* 16.2)

The same Midrash interprets the words of the bride in the Song of Songs: "I sleep but my heart is awake" (5:2) in this way:

> I sleep — in lack of redemption;
> Yet the heart [of the Holy One] is awake to
>   redeem me.

It even goes so far as to say that in Psalm 73:26 "the Holy One is actually identified as the heart of Israel" for it reads the verse, "God the rock of my heart and my portion forever" as "God [is] the rock, my heart, and my portion forever" (*Piska* 5.6).

The midrashic world is part of the unknown Judaism. Few Christians today, and not many Jews, realize its wealth, its diverse approaches to God, and its offers of an outpouring of His love. These are two pleas to the people of Israel, as given in the *Pesikta de Rab Kahana* from which I just quoted:

> Make for me an opening in you,
>> an opening as narrow as the eye of a needle,
> and I will make it so wide
>> that camps full of soldiers and huge engines
>>> can enter.
>
> Vow repentance for as little time
>> as it takes to wink an eye,
> "and you will be aware
>> that I am the Lord [of mercy] (Ps 46:11)."
>>>> (*Piska* 24:12)

In my search for a vision that Jews and Christians can share, I am sustained by no less a scholar of various midrashic works than Rabbi William G. Braude. In his introduction to the *Pesikta de Rab Kahana*, he voices the hope that it (together, we may add, with other *midrashim*) will serve as a bridge, a bridge between Jewish past and the Jewish present, a bridge between Jewish thought and the world's understanding of Judaism, a bridge between Jews and all those who are not Jews but share with them the heritage of Jewish Scripture and the teaching of the Rabbis.[30]

JEWISH AND CHRISTIAN THEOLOGIES

Lest my search for a basic vision, one common to Jewish and Christian ways, be taken as a search for the lowest common denominator, I would like to compare the two theologies very briefly. I detest the glossing over of differences, yet I am no less averse to an unwarranted widening of trenches. There can be no doubt that Jews and Christians, true to their authentic traditions, share the vision of God being involved in human affairs in a loving, though mysterious and, therefore, not always comprehensible way. Still, they differ in some important particulars. For normative Judaism, there is one great saving event, the Exodus, and one great revelatory moment, God's summons of Israel at Mt. Sinai. For Christians, too, the Exodus and the revelation from Sinai (as well as that from the thornbush) are of fundamental significance, but they are crowned by the Christ event. In Christ, the Christian believes all repentant sinners are saved, and through Him, human beings the world over are addressed by God.

A Jew may well see in Jesus a certain climax. With Joseph Klausner he may perceive in him a "great teacher of morality," an "artist in the telling of parables."[31] Or he may say with Rabbi Leo Baeck that Jesus was "a Jew among Jews [whom] Jewish history and Jewish reflection may not pass by, may not ignore. Since he was, no time has been without him; nor has there been a time that has not been challenged by [him]."[32] The Christian, however, does not stop here. In Jesus, Son of Abraham, Son of David, a Christian believes God entered human history in a way incomparable to all His former visitations. In Christ, YHVH, the everpresent Lord who had pledged to love His people always, pitched His tent among us. He is thus Immanuel, "God with us" (Mt 1:23). Other titles of sovereignty are "the Image of the Invisible God" (Col 1:15), "the *philanthropia* of God, His love of humanity, made manifest" (Tit 3:4), "the Word become flesh" (Jn 1:14). These are but a few that show how the New Testament writers experienced Him, and how Christians through the centuries have known and loved Him.[33]

As God's *philanthropia* — His love of Man embodied — Jesus is the Savior, the Reconciler, the Pardoner. He bore the burden of our sins, of everyone's sins, the Christian believes. He made the pain and burden of every human being His own. He suffered and died for others. So essential are His vicarious suffering and redeeming death to the Christian faith that without them there is no gospel. A Christian who denies that Jesus bore the cross and died on it out of love for all ceases to be one. A Jew who maintains that vicarious suffering is an altogether un-Jewish idea and, therefore unacceptable, is wrong, but he or she remains a Jew.

AGGADIC TEACHING

Rabbinic thought proclaiming that God suffers with and for His people is part of aggadic teaching. The portion of rabbinic lore that does not deal with laws and regulations — *halakhah* — is called *aggadah*. It encompasses biblical interpretation and theological speculation, history and legend, moral teaching and prayers, reproofs and consolations of the people, expressions of messianic hope, maxims, witticisms, stories of all kinds, and other features. No wonder that *aggadah* is commonly called "non-binding," that is, not a matter of belief. It has been said that some of its interpretations obey the creative skill, the fancy of the one who offers them, and are not part of Torah, not part of the (obligatory) Tradition.[34]

If all one remembers about aggadic teaching is its non-impelling character, one may well shove the rabbis' view on God's self-abandonment aside as mere talk, unable to end or even lessen the anguish of victims or survivors. But, if one agrees with Abraham J. Heschel that "to reduce Judaism to law, to halacha, is to dim its light, to pervert its essence and kill its spirit,"[35] one cannot look upon rabbinic sayings on God's infinite pity as "empty words of a dream (Robert Bridges)." Heschel sees in Judaism an inner polarity at work, and thus a need for both *halakhah* and *aggadah*:

> Halacha deals with details, with each command-
> ment separately; agada with the whole of life,
> with the totality of religious life... Halacha gives
> us norms for action; agada, the vision of the ends
> of living... Halacha decrees, agada inspires.[36]

Once one accepts Heschel's perspective, one cannot treat the rabbinic vision of God as Israel's kin, the One who feels the pain of His people as His own, as if it were a fairy tale. Far from being make-believe, the narratives of the rabbis take us to the heart of things.

A Common Origin

To return to the differences between Jewish and Christian beliefs, the rather obvious ones I touched upon before are not the only ones to separate the latter from the former. True, at the core of rabbinic Judaism and the New Testament message is this common assurance that God, whose abode is the infinite and eternal glory of Heaven, "descended" to earth out of love. He chose the smallest spot in this universe for the purpose of serving His people, saving them, sharing their pain, pronouncing His oneness with them, in word and deed. Yet, Jews and Christians differ in their views on how this wonder of divine compassion was enacted. Peter Kuhn points out that rabbinic faith sees nature and person in God as one. When God humbles Himself, it is the one divine person who humbles Himself. According to the Christian faith, God is Triune. When God humbled Himself to take on human nature, it was the Son, the Second Person of the Trinity, who assumed a mortal frame.[37]

The coincidence or correspondence of nature and person in God, carries with it a danger, Kuhn insists. In Christian theology, the vis-a-vis of Father and Son preserves God's freedom and sovereignty, even when He abases Himself. In rabbinic thought, however, it appears, at times, as if God entered the world so totally, as if He subjected Himself to its dimensions, conditions, and history so entirely that His free will, too, seems subordinate to them. His freely chosen self-abandonment has almost turned into a passive attitude toward the world so that its redemption becomes His own redemption.[38]

Whatever one thinks of Kuhn's attempt to compare (and consequently contrast) Jewish and Christian theologies; whatever their disparities, they are akin. They are, I have no doubt, closely related. Indeed, belief in God's self-effacement and His suffering with and for His creatures separates Judaism and Christianity from the many world religions. Their kinship is deeper still. There are definite indications that some rabbinic views on God's humility are older than the compilations in which they appear; older even than the rabbis whose names they bear. In substance, they may go back to the first century A.D. or even to times before that. I am bold enough to say that it was early rabbinic thought that helped shape the New Testament perceptions on vicarious suffering, rather than some hellenistic notion or oriental cultic observance, as the scholarly vogue of yesteryear maintained. I am convinced that both theologies have their origin in ancient Israel, and that the common ground I have been looking for is, thus, as firm as rock.

VII
THE ANSWER OF FAITH

In Their Daring, then, the Jewish sages teach: When Israel hurts, the Holy One, blessed be He, hurts too. The living God identifies Himself with the sufferer. Am I a dreamer when I think that the teachings with which the ancient rabbis sought to answer Israel's grief over Jerusalem's destruction and the people's exile have something to tell the anguished men and women of today? Have I fallen easy prey to wishful thinking when I assume that the rabbinic and Christian visions of God's self-effacement, however much they may differ, are sufficiently close to allow Jews and Christians — Jewish and Christian theologians in particular — to attempt a common response to the question that has elicited this essay?

LEAP OF FAITH

The quest for a common response is no romantic illusion; neither is the vision of the rabbis. Yet, both call for an act of faith. The most moving statement by a modern Jewish thinker on such a leap of faith is by Michael Wyschogrod:

> The basic message of Judaism is that God is a redeeming God. No proof is needed for this assertion; it is self-evident. It is the basic message of Psalms as it is of the Eighteen Benedictions. There we speak of God as the "shield of Abraham," "who builds Jerusalem," "who gathers the dispersed of Israel," "who heals the sick of Israel," "who resurrects the dead" and so on and so on. All of these are acts of redemption. The basic message of the Eighteen Benedictions is that God is a redeeming God, no matter what, and irrespective of how convincing the evidence

51

to the contrary is. Jews have prayed to God "who heals the sick of Israel" after coming home from the funeral of someone loved. They saw that God does not heal all the sick of Israel. Nevertheless, they recited the blessing. The facts had to yield to the proclamation of faith. God was a redeeming God. He heals the sick of Israel. And if it does not seem so, then we just repeat the formula: he heals the sick of Israel. He said he heals them and he does heal them. He will heal them. We can trust him. His promises are not made in vain. They will be fulfilled because he is a redeeming God.[39]

INFINITE COMPASSION

Once this wonder of faith has invaded our lives, we can boldly answer the question that our hearts ask in fear and trembling: "Where was God when the gas ovens of Auschwitz worked full blast?" With the same throbbing heart, we answer: "God was with the victims." With them, He walked the stations of their pain: He endured degradation, as the victims were "shipped" to the "East" — a euphemism for crematoria — like cattle, indeed worse than cattle. His heart was wrenched at the hour of parting when families were torn asunder, when those assigned to hard labor were separated from those to be fed instantly to the Moloch of hate. He was humbled in all their humiliations. He shared the agony of their last minutes, as they struggled against the deadly poison.

"Can anyone take comfort from the thought of a God helplessly stumbling toward gas chambers?" a listener to a lecture of mine wondered. Of course not. But the vision of God suffering with and for the persecuted is not one of divine impotence. A terrified animal that is being dragged to the slaughterhouse is defenseless, left to the rough hands of its butcher. God, however, free and sovereign, is totally devoted to the salvation of men, women, and children —

52

even though His way of saving us does not always mean instantaneous rescue and, more often than not, demands our partnership. His compassion is infinite; like all true compassion, it is strength, not weakness.

FAITH RESTORED

The Lord also triumphed with Hitler's victims as some proclaimed aloud their faith, turning seeming defeat into victory. Sholem Asch seems to have been the first in the West to testify to the glorious end of believers among the prisoners of the Warsaw ghetto. Quoting from a manifesto of underground forces, he describes how devout Jews, breathing their last, called out: *Shema Yisrael*, "Hear, O Israel, the Lord our God, the Lord is One," while pious Catholics died with the names of Jesus and Mary on their lips. Sholem Asch then adds: "I do not believe that since Nero these two calls have been mingled together in an arena of martyrdom."[40] True, the Christian victims in Auschwitz and other domains of Moloch were few when compared to their many Jewish brethren. Still, in the extermination camps, the prayers of Jews and Christians rose together, and were heard together by the living God.

Recently, an extraordinary testimony of faith born in one of the Nazi death camps was broadcast by the B.B.C.. Rabbi Hugo Gryn, vice-president of Leo Baeck College, the rabbinical seminary of liberal Judaism in England, told how, as a youngster imprisoned in a Nazi concentration camp, he discovered God. Not the God of his childhood, he stressed; that God he had lost, or rather lost sight of, in the presence of the four crematoria of Auschwitz. He had implored God "to do something"; when nothing happened, he turned his back on Him. Later, in one of the forced labor camps, as he perceived more clearly the various ways by which the human mind can respond to people and to events, he rediscovered the living God. Though the constant rumors that American troops would come and liberate the inmates proved to be wishful thinking; though he was disappointed again and again, he held on to the conviction that in the end evil would be vanquished.[41]

Movingly, he related how song, that elemental utterance of the human spirit, had sustained him in the deadly monotony of camp life. While pushing a cart filled with human excrement, or carrying a sack of cement from one spot to another, he sang — rather he hummed to himself so as not be heard by the guards — the twelfth principle of the Jewish faith, as Maimonides saw and expressed it:

Ani ma'amin...,

With perfect faith, I believe in the coming of the Messiah; even though he tarry, daily will I await his coming.

His faith, he explained, was a blend of trust and hope. With God and man working together, salvation was possible; redemption in this world, here and now, was more than a pious dream. There was nothing to fear in this world, he proclaimed, but God.[42]

FEAR OF GOD

In biblical speech, "fear of God" is fear of His judgment, fear of chastisement. Yet, it is also, even more intensely, the awareness of God's awesome nature, His majesty. In rabbinical language, fear of God is akin to the love of Him. Yet, "there is nothing to fear in this world but God" is not a claim we hear every day. It is more likely that people ask, as Martin Buber puts it: In a world as cruel, as ghastly as that of the Holocaust, one can still believe in God, but is life with Him possible? Can one still speak to a God who allowed Auschwitz to happen? Can one call on Him?[43] Others, like Irving Greenberg, think that after Auschwitz all we are left with are "moment faiths," "moments when Redeemer and the vision of redemption are present, interspersed with times when the flames and smoke of the burning children blot out faith — though it flickers again."[44]

I have no desire to argue here with those who so think. It would be an argument across charred bodies, indeed, a desert of ashes. Still, I must say that neither my mind nor my heart can grasp the two statements. Buber rightly holds that faith is never the mere acceptance of a proposition, the proposition that "God exists." Faith is trust, the surrender of one's being, devotion, love. But if this be so, how can anyone believe in God and *not* call on Him? Faith compels the believer to pray, to turn to Him. Greenberg's view is equally puzzling. Perhaps, he simply meant that though we cling to God, we may still be tempted by doubts, or walk through times of darkness; none could disagree. But, Greenberg is saying something else: "Faith is a moment of truth, but there are moments when it is not true."[45] Unless "true" were to mean something like instantly convincing or spellbinding, faith could not possibly be now true, now untrue.

FAITH: FREE OR FETTERED

Quite different, however, is the feeling of having been abandoned by God. It may overcome the purest, the most faithful. The violent complaint of one wrongly persecuted, at the beginning of Psalm 22, which Jesus made His own on the cross, is evidence of different moments of faith: faith free and victorious, and faith fettered by unspeakable pain. It was such pain that exploded in the cry: "God, my God, why have you forsaken me?" (Mk 15:34; Mt 27:46). Or, as a modern rendering puts it:

> I cry out, and you stay away.
> My God, I call all day — you are silent.
> I call through the night, and you just let me call.[46]

Still, the one stricken and abandoned by all has no friend to go to but the silent, seemingly absent, God. Thus — oh wonder of perseverance! — the psalmist's lament turns into thanksgiving and joy (see Ps 22:23-27). Even into the great promise: "I will live for you" (v. 31).[47]

55

I do not take suffering lightly; the mere thought of someone in great pain makes me shudder. Yet, no human suffering through the ages will, I trust, keep me from professing: "I believe in the living God, present in all human hells, compassionate, and loving." On the contrary, I hope, it will always lead me to affirm Him with power and passion. Without that faith, human sorrow — in particular the desolation of Auschwitz — would be unbearable. Moreover, modern Man's arrogance, one of the factors that begot Hitler with his hatred of everything Jewish, Christian, and human, is also the cause of modern unbelief or belief in an absent, non-caring deity.

BROTHERHOOD OF HOPE

When human beings appoint themselves the center of things; when they consider themselves no longer stewards but masters of the world, indeed, little gods; when all possessions, actual and potential, are regarded theirs by right; when everything seems within reach; when men and women are their own managers in all they do; when everything appears possible, possible without divine help, genuine faith must wither away. Even though the self-assurance of twentieth century Man spells disaster — the present pollution of soil, water, and air is evidence of the debacle of that self-aggrandizement — it will not yield, it seems, either to common sense or the venture of faith.

Were I to join the chorus of those who preach a maimed and maiming faith, I would prolong the life of Hitler's ideology. Faith is a stronger protest against the Fuhrer's spirit — partly alive in some of those who detest him — than all rhetoric. A moment ago, I spoke of R. Gryn's profession of faith uttered in one of Hitler's hells:

> With perfect faith, I believe in the coming of the Messiah; even though he tarry, daily will I await his coming.

This is the one before last of Maimonides' principles of the Jewish faith. The last one proclaims:

> With perfect faith I believe that the dead will
> rise, at a time pleasing to the Creator, blessed be
> His name.

While Jews pray thus, Christians express hope in the return of the Christ. They, too, expect the triumph of life or rather the triumph of God. Indeed, all Christians creeds conclude with words like these:

> We look for the resurrection of the dead
> and the life of the world to come. Amen.

Again, Jews and Christians bear a similar witness, and meet in a unique fellowship, the brotherhood of hope.

VIII
A FINAL WORD

I BEGAN THESE reflections with the clear, unequivocal statement that the Holocaust is unique. The murder of six millions Jews by the Hitler-inspired industry of hatred is not just another instance of that cruelty which defaces so much of human history. It is not merely part of that rage which has been described in these words: *Homo homini lupus*, freely translated: "Human beings behave like wolves toward other human beings." In the wanton murder of Jewish men, women, and children a *new* ideology was at work, no matter how many roots it may have had in past notions or abuses. A *new* method of exterminating people was in operation, no matter how many models of killing one's fellow the world had seen. A *new* goal was set. The new murderers did not madly thirst for blood; with cool mind and steady hand, they decreed the doom of a whole people.

To this new phenomenon and the question it raises about God's governance and the world's evil, I have tried to give in these pages, not a new but an old answer, one that assumes freshness and youth, as soon as it is lived. For some writers on the Holocaust, however, the lasting truths of faith are suspect. It has been said that Auschwitz put the God of Israel in the dock. After all, He created the world, thus bearing ultimate responsibility for the evil in it. Again, He gave Israel that fatal gift of the covenant. Not only is it the root of all Jewish suffering, it has also served God as a tool of oppression. With its aid, He has kept His people chained to Himself. Hence the covenant, as it has been understood up to now, must be abrogated and God, as accomplice to all the crimes against Jews, do penance. All those who speak thus are, without realizing it, echoers of Hitler's shrill voice.

Everything has been tainted by the Holocaust, everything has become dated, we are told. Hence what *is* must give way to something that is *not yet*. We need a new Torah, a new revelation. Traditional Christology must yield to a novel one, one even without the Christ. Since suffering is wicked, all thought of the crucifixion must be banished; indeed, since the proclamation of Christ's resurrection did not make crime impossible, belief in it may have to cease, too. Again, the Church must forego her claims. It is worth noticing that all these "revolutionary" demands call for a change in institutions, a rethinking of articles of faith, but never a call for an inner renewal of people, of Christians as well as Jews, as did Christ and the prophets before Him. The suffering of the six millions must never be a shield behind which we can hide.

Some maintain that after Auschwitz faith in God is no longer possible; others hold that the soul can at best shuttle from assent to dissent or denial, swing from trust to the lack of it. Through Auschwitz, hope, devotion became vain attempts. All God-talk has become senseless, since the preaching of the Word of God did not prevent the most horrible crimes. For a time, we should refrain from uttering the divine Name, rather give all our energy to the building of a truly human society, in which men and women can, indeed, are impelled to live as "images of God." I find these "new rationalizations" warring not only against God but against reason itself. If God failed us; if He deceived His people; if He coldly abandoned Hitler's victims to doom, how can we still speak of human beings as having been created in God's image?

I respect the inner turmoil suffered by many writers at the sight of evil men as well as evil deeds, and their difficulty in understanding the ways of God. Were I to join these writers and make their doctrines my own, I would harm all those whose hearts ache: I would swing a deadly axe instead of extending a healing hand. Moreover, I would commit spiritual suicide for I could not live without the God who speaks and demands my response, to whom I may speak, and who hears me. Would that all who have been touched by the terror of Auschwitz could pray with the great Hebrew poet and philosopher of eleventh century Spain, Solomon Ibn Gabirol:

59

O my God,...

Were I not to yearn for Your compassion.
  who but You would take pity on me?
Even though You were to slay me,
  I would yet trust You.

Were You to visit me with affliction,
  I would flee from You to Yourself.
From Your anger I will take cover
  under the shadow of Your Presence.

To the hem of Your compassion I will cling
  till You show me love.
I will not let You go,
  unless You bless me.[48]

Notes

1. Elie Wiesel, *One Generation After* New York: Random House, 1970), p. 181.

2. See Rahner-Vorgrimler, *Theological Dictionary* (New York: Herder & Herder, 1965), p. 351.

3. One cannot repeat often enough that by itself the vast number of murdered victims does not make the Holocaust the consummate evil it is. Yet, my contention needs to be marked off from another set of opinions. "Opinions" may be too mild a term for various schemes to obliterate the memory of Hitler's crimes against Jews. Some try to lower the figure of six million to a considerable degree; others present the Holocaust as a minor incident of World War II, something like a skirmish between two hostile camps; still others deny its existence altogether. The tales of mass murder, the latter say, are nothing but stories put out by enemy propaganda.

It is a trick of the heart, common to all of us, to defend ourselves, even at the expense of truth, to justify our actions with all the artistry we can muster, or to pretend that we are free of any guilt. We engage in such cover-up whether the sins to be concealed are our personal ones or those of our group. The advocates of Nazi innocence, however, have not succumbed to this *common* temptation. In their perversity, they not only maintain that the massacre never took place, they also shift the blame for the plot of liquidating a whole people from Hitler and his henchmen to the Jews: Not the murderers were and are guilty, but those murdered by them.

By calling the story of the death camps a "hoax" as I have indicated in the introduction to this essay, the defenders of Nazi innocence carry on the vilification of Jews that many people thought had ended for good. With tongue or pen, they try to slay those whom Himmler's arm had been unable to reach. At the same time, their denial of the horror of gas ovens is an attempt to keep intact the heroic mantle the

61

rulers of the Third Reich had cloaked their Jew-hatred in. The anti-Jewish ideology and practice of the Nazis is thus shown to be not only a crime but also a sham, a fraud.

For all these reasons, an exact count of the Nazi murders of Jews is of great importance. To my knowledge, the first and only attempt by a Christian to compile the statistics of Nazi terror against Jews in English is by my late colleague, Fr. William Keller. (See Keller, "Ledger of Death" *The Bridge*, ed. John M. Oesterreicher (New York: Pantheon, 1955) I, pp. 283-291.

On the thirty-third anniversary of the collapse of the Third Reich, the Center of Documentation of Nazi War Crimes in Haifa made public a sworn statement by Wilhelm Hoettl, *Sturmbannfuehrer* or major in the SS, made in Nuremberg on November 26, 1945. In it, he tells of a report Adolf Eichmann had to make to SS-chief Heinrich Himmler, on the number of Jews killed. Four million, he related to Himmler, were gassed in the various extermination camps, while two million were shot by special commandos during the Nazi invasion of Russia. Himmler was dissatisfied with Eichmann's account; based on other information, he was convinced that the figure of Jews murdered exceeded six million. (See *The Jerusalem post*, International Edition, May 16, 1978.)

4. For the full text and the bibliographical reference, see Edward A. Synan, *The Popes and the Jews in the Middle Ages* (New York: Macmillan, 1965), pp. 75, 208.

5. See Hermann Rauschning, *The Voice of Destruction* (New York: Putman, 1940), pp. 223-228.

6. *Ibid.*, p. 241.

7. Friedrich Wilhelm Nietzsche, *The Twilight of Idols*, VII. p. 4.

8. Nietzsche, *The Antichrist*, 21, 17.

9. Julian Green, "Journal," *Revue de Paris*, June, 1949.

10. Nuremberg Military Tribunals, "Trials of War Criminals" (Washington, D.C., 1952), XII, 432ff. (No. 1805).

11. See Thomas and Margaret Melady, *Idi Amin Dada, Hitler in Africa*, (Kansas City: Sheed, Andrews, etc., 1977).

12. Nelly Sachs, *O The Chimneys*, Selected poems in a bilingual edition (New York: Farrar, Straus, and Giroux, 1967), p. 3.

13. *Ibid.*, p. 7.

14. *Ibid*, pp. 314, 387. In "Some Theological Reflections on the Holocaust," Michael Wyschogrod views literary presentation of the Holocaust inappropriate. He writes: "Art takes the sting out of suffering. It transforms suffering into a catharsis for which people are willing to pay money to experience... But no such catharsis can be derived from the Holocaust. It must remain life and not art. It is therefore forbidden to make fiction of the Holocaust." (*Response*, A Contemporary Jewish Review [Spring 1975] p. 68.) Without wishing to discuss Prof. Wyschogrod's scorn for art as entertainment only, and his disapproval of it as groping for what hides behind the obvious, I do not think that Nelly Sach's verse comes under his interdict. It is hardly her intention to idealize the Holocaust, to transfigure its abhorrence into something pretty or pleasurable. If one is to assign to her work — the genuine outpourings of a grieving heart, though not in the language of every day — a purpose, it is that of keeping grief from turning into despair.

15. Zvi Kolitz's story was first published in a Buenos Aires Yiddish weekly in 1946. It has since appeared in several languages. For an English translation, see Elizabeth Orsten, "Light in Darkness," *The Bridge*, ed. J.M. Oesterreicher, (New York: Pantheon, 1958) III, pp. 325-339.

16. *Ibid.*, p. 329.

17. *Ibid.*, pp. 332-333.

18. *Ibid.*, p. 335.

19. For detailed information on *Shevet Yehudah*, see "Ibn Verga, Solomon" in *Encyclopedia Judaica* (New York: Macmillan, 1971) V, p. 1203.

20. *Pesikta Rabbati*, piska 30, ed. Friedmann, p. 142a, English translation in *Pesikta Rabbati*, trans. William G. Braude (New Haven: Yale University Press, 1968) II, 596.

21. *Piska* was originally the term for the biblical portion to be read on a certain day of the liturgical year. Eventually, this designation was extended to a biblical discourse on a given lesson. All the discourses of the year came to be called *Pesikata* or *Pesikta*. *Pesikta Rabbati* is then "The great collection (anthology) of the discourses on the lessons of the year."

22. From a personal communication. Rabbi Petuchowski stresses "(a) that the 'argument' has not been finally settled and (b) that catastrophes like the Holocaust tend to re-open the 'argument' time and again."

23. *Ibid.*

24. For Braude's translation, which I have followed in part, see *Pesikta R.*, II, p. 672. The confession of sins quoted in *Piska* 35 is paralleled by the one recited during the *Amidah* of the *Yom Kippur* service.

25. Some clarification may be advisable on the meaning of "humility," as used in this context. The singer of Psalm 18 extols his God for having delivered him from the hands of those who sought his life. In verse 36, he sings: "Your humility — *'anevatekha* — makes me great." Commonly, humility denotes the deferential attitude of a person of lower toward one of higher rank. In this verse, however, it tells of the Creator's bending down to His creature. Some transla-

tors avoid the paradox of a humble God by saying "gentleness," "care," or "help" instead of "humility." Others substitute for humility another word or phrase that implies the Lord's "lowering" Himself, His "leaning" toward His children. The older version of the JPS has "Your condescension," Buber reads *deine Beugung,* 'your bowing down," NAB says "You stooped down to make me great." Many rabbinic texts quoted here revolve about the mystery of the humble God. Peter Kuhn (see note 29) renders the concept *'anevetanut* with *Selbsterniedrigung* ("Self-humbling"). I myself prefer to call the divine humility "self-abandonment" or "self-effacement" — two words that seem to express best God's movement toward His elect, His loving identification with their destiny.

26. R. Yohanan finds God's solitary grandeur and His bending down to His creatures juxtaposed in all three divisions of the Hebrew Scriptures: the Torah, the Prophets, and Sacred Writings. In Deuteronomy 10:17, God is portrayed as "the Lord of lords" and the "Protector of the powerless." In Isaiah 57:15, God is called the High and Exalted, the Holy and Eternal One, as well as the "One who dwells with the broken-hearted and humble in spirit." In Psalm 68:5, the Lord is extolled as the One "who rides upon the clouds" and as "the Father of orphans and Defender of widows."

27. The reading "heart of the burning bush" is based on the kind of rearrangement of letters the rabbis are fond of. The actual texts say that God was "in the flame, *be-libat,* of the bush." One commentator reads instead, 'God appeared in the heart, *be-libo,* of the bush."

28. The seven biblical passages recalled by R. Eleazar b. Pedat are Dt 10:17f; Is 57:15; 66:1f; Ps 10:16f; Ps 68:5f; Ps 138:6; Ps 146:67.

29. Peter Kuhn, *Gottes Selbsterniedrigung in der Theologie der Rabbinen* (Munich: Koesel, 1968), p. 85.

30. *Pesikta de Rab Kahana,* trans. Braude-Kapstein (Philadelphia: Jewish Publication Society, 1975) p. xvi.

31. Joseph Klausner, *Jesus von Nazareth* (New York: Macmillan, 1943) p. 414.

32. Leo Baeck, "The Gospel as a Document of the History of the Jewish Faith," in *Judaism and Christianity* (New York: Atheneum, 1970) p. 101.

33. It is commonly held that the mere thought of God-in-the-flesh is unbearable to the Jewish mind. Trude Weiss-Rosmarin, for instance, claims: "The Unity of God, sacred to Judaism beyond all else, is utterly irreconcilable... with the belief in incarnation." (*Judaism and Christianity* (New York: Jonathan David, 1968), p. 21.) No matter how often repeated and how widely accepted, a stereotype is never more than an oversimplified notion. One needs only recall the theophany at Mamre to realize that such a thesis is far too rigid. Scripture tells that God appeared to Abraham, and that Abraham saw "three men standing before him" (Gn 18:2). However one explains this divine visit, it cannot be fitted into a simplistic frame.

True, Jewish tradition does not acknowledge the mystery of God-*become*-man. Midrashic literature speaks of God *having* a human form, though one of heavenly dimension and resplendent with glory. At the time of the Exodus, God is said to have appeared in Israel's midst as Man. *Exodus Rabbah* speaks of the birth of a Hebrew child under the oppressive rule of a hostile Pharaoh as an event requiring divine assistance. A Hebrew woman in labor, would go to the fields and be delivered ("under an appletree," *b Sot* 11b, echoing Ct 8:5). As soon as the baby was born, the mother would entrust it to the Lord: "Lord of the Universe, I have done my part; now you do yours." Immediately, the Lord would descend in His glory, cut the umbilical cord, wash and anoint the new-born babe. The children are said to have grown up in the field. When they finally came home, they were asked: "Who looked after you?" Their answer was: "A fine handsome young man came down and attended to all our needs, as it says: 'My lover is radiant and ruddy, pre-eminent above ten thousands' (Ct 5:10)." In later years, as

He crossed the Sea with Moses, the children now grown up recognized God as the One who cared for them when they were little (*Ex. r.* 23, 8). According to *bSot* 11b the midwifely service is rendered, not by God, but by a heavenly messenger.

When the Egyptians were miraculously thwarted in their attempt to return the Israelites to forced labor, Moses and his own are said to have sung: "The Lord is a Man of War, the Lord is His name" (Ex 15:3). We are wont to take "man of war" or "warrior" as a metaphor. The *Mekhilta*, however, seems to understand "warrior" more concretely, not to say literally. There, we are told that at the Sea of Reeds the Lord appeared "like a mighty hero with a sword," "a spear," "a shield and buckler," "with a coat of mail and helmet." At Sinai, the Midrash goes on, He did not show Himself in youthful vigor, but as "an old man full of mercy" for it is clearly said: "And they saw the God of Israel" (Ex 24:10). It is exactly this latter verse that identifies the One who bore the marks of old age, wisdom and compassion, with the One true God. Thus, the *Mekhilta* continues, Scripture provides "no excuse for the nations for saying that there are two powers (incidentally, a Gnostic, not a Christian doctrine) but declares: 'The Lord is a Man of War, the Lord is His name.' He, it is who was in Egypt, and He was at the sea. It is He who was in the past and He who will be in the future. It is He who is in this world and He who will be in the world to come." *(Mekh.*, "Shirata" IV; *Mekilta de R. Ishmael*, J. Lauterbach ed. [Philadelphia: J.P.S., 1933] II, 31f.)

It is difficult to categorize rabbinic speech about the humanity of God. It seems to be more than metaphoric, yet not entirely factual. In *Pesikta Rabbati* 14, 10 it is said that the power of the Prophets is great for they liken the figure of Omnipotence above to the figure of human beings below. In R. Braude's translation, the corresponding lines read: "Very wise in the power of language are the Prophets who in figurative terms speak of the likeness of the Almighty as though of the likeness of a man, as is said, 'And I heard the voice of a Man' (Dan 8:16). R. Yudan bar Simon said: There is another verse which uses figurative terms even more boldly: "And upon the likeness of the throne was a likeness as the appearance of a Man above upon it (Ez 1:26)." (Braude, *Pesikta Rabbati*, I, 279.) I do not desire to determine the nature of the rabbinic allusions to God's humanity, nor do I feel competent to do so. All I wish to accomplish is to gainsay precipitous, simplistic judgments on the differences between Judaism and Christianity.

34. For fuller information on the nature and role of *aggadah* see *Encyclopedia Judaica* (New York: Macmillan, 1971) II, 354-366 or *The Encyclopedia of the Jewish Religion* (New York: Holt, Rinehart and Winston, 1965), p.15-17.

35. Abraham Joshua Heschel, *God in Search of Man* (New York: Farrar, Straus and Cudahy, 1951), p. 338. See also the selection of Heschel's writings by Fritz A. Rothschild, *Between God and Man* (New York: The Free Press, 1965), p.176.

36. Heschel, *ibid.*, p. 336-337; Rothschild, *ibid.*, p. 175.

37. Kuhn, *Gottes Selbsterniedrigung* p. 106.

38. *Ibid.*

39. Wyschogrod, "Theological Reflections," *loc. cit.* pp 66-67.

40. Sholem Asch, "In the Valley of Death," *The New York Times Magazine*, February 7, 1943.

41. R. Gryn's radio meditations were published in the magazine *European Judaism*, a copy of which I have not been able to obtain. I am following the French translation, "Quatre meditations sur la souffrance," *Information Juive* (Paris) November, 1977.

42. *Ibid.*

43. Martin Buber, "The Dialogue between Heaven and Earth," in *At the Turning, Three Addresses on Judaism* (New York: Farrar, Straus and Young, 1952) p. 61.

44. Irving Greenberg, "Theological Reflections on the Holocaust," *Auschwitz: Beginning of a New Era?* ed. Eva Fleischner (New York: KTAV. 1977) p. 27.

45. *Ibid.* p. 33.

46. Huub Oosterhuis and others, *Fifty Psalms, An Attempt at a New Translation* (New York: Herder and Herder, 1969) p. 32.

47. If one listens to Jesus' cry with only half an ear, one hears but utter desolation, sheer despair. Yet, if one listens intensely, one encounters a twofold attitude. On the one hand, Jesus gives voice to His extreme loneliness: He has been deserted by His companions, deprived of human fellowship; He even feels abandoned by His Father. On the other hand, at the moment of deepest distress, of an unmatched darkness of the soul — it is as if His Father had withdrawn His presence, as if He were far away, deaf to His cries for help, to His wails and groans (See Ps 22:2b) — Jesus maintains His trust. Despite His experience of being all alone in His struggle, He holds fast to His Father. However intense His pain, however oppressive the darkness of His soul, He does not rebel, accuse, or challenge the Father. He lovingly calls Him *Eli, Eli, "my* God, *my* God."

It cannot be said often enough that Jesus' cry: "My God, my God, why have you forsaken me?" is not an isolated saying but the opening line of Psalm 22, a song that begins in a mood of defeat but ends with one of victory. I have no doubt that as Jesus intoned that initial line, the entire psalm was present to His heart; in His mind He may even have continued saying it from the words of seeming abandonment to those of vindication. Moreover, the anguished cry is only one of the last words of Jesus the evangelists record. While the Fourth Gospel has Him say: "It (my errand of mercy) is accomplished" (19:30), Luke has Him promise paradise to a changed rebel against the Roman yoke (23:43) and die with the joyous commitment: "Into Your hands I entrust my spirit" (23:46, see Ps 31:6.)

48. I bear responsibility for this translation. For the original text and the noted translation of this and other poems of Ibn Gabirol by Israel Zangwil, see the bilingual edition of *Selected Religious Poems by Solomon Ibn Gabirol*, ed. Israel Davidson (Philadelphia: JPSA, 1974, paperback) p. 118.

AFTERWORD

A prophet is one who turns mystery into music, looks to the future and replies to the present through the past. David in his psalms sang of the secrets of God's love for His people and Isaiah allowed past promises of the Messiah to respond to the present problems of a king. Both saw the Kingdom of God to come. One is reminded of such a prophetic approach in this very learned and sensitive essay in which Msgr. John M. Oesterreicher addresses the horror of the Holocaust.

The paradox of a good God allowing bad people to inflict awesome anguish upon His chosen ones — those whom He even loves as His children — is a deep mystery which only the most courageous seek to address. A person with a prophetic view may see it as unsolvable. He must press on, nonetheless, even if to do so is to do no more than to deepen the darkness. Is it not in this darkness of things unseen that only strong faith can provide the glimmer of light which dispels despair and forms the foundation for the hope of a solution?

The cruel question of, "Where were you, my God, when I needed you?" echoes plaintively through the narratives of both Testaments. It came from the lips of Moses as he cried out to YHVH in the desert. It reverberates again centuries later. The sealed tomb of Lazarus was the setting for Martha's tearful plea to her Galilean friend, "If only you had been here, Lord." Neither Judaism nor Christianity holds a monopoly on the need to describe this hurt and to wonder about the hell that comes from a lack of divine healing.

With a kind of prophetic hindsight, Msgr. Oesterreicher has guided his readers on a quest for the answer to Auschwitz and has taken them over a path crisscrossed with the imprints of both reason and revelation. His ultimate conclusion is a stunning blend of both.

Has the mystery of God's presence or absence in the history of Holocaust been definitively answered? Honesty demands that the answer must be, "No." A study of this excellent essay does show, however, some of the pieces of the answer. We must read them now as "through a glass darkly," and leave the complete explanation for that moment when we shall experience Divine Providence "face to face." We recognize, at the same time, that much of the darkness has been dissipated by the logic and love which Msgr. Oesterreicher brings to his interpretation and instruction.

No prophet claims to understand perfectly all of the aspects of the divine providential plan he preaches. Patient analysis does point out the elements and even the contradictions with which he must deal. This process, John Oesterreicher has carried out extremely well. No difficulty is sidestepped. No apparent contradiction is ignored.

The pieces of the divinely human puzzle which must be put together in order to explain God's presence at the Holocaust are jagged indeed. To the earthly eye they seem simply not to fit. But the prophet has more than an earthly eye. He sees as perfectly logical people singing in the midst of misery. He perceives as profoundly plausible that a father could see his children suffer, and by his presence with them participate in their pain. He understands with the ancient Israelites that only faith forms a key to unlock these mysteries. Sometimes the law of love must bolster the rules of logic if we are to give answer to that most gnawing of all questions, "Why?"

Divine reason, mystery, logic and love, music and misery — these are concepts with which our contemporary society would rather not deal. They can be unrewarding, unpleasant, and unclear. Our world all too often encourages us to be self-forgiving of those times when our solution to a problem is simply to forget it. As long as there are people like John Oesterreicher, who insist that we unmask myths and fight the folly of those who try to make the past not to have been, our unsettling search for truth is made more secure.

The horror of the Holocaust is not the only desecration which some seek to deny. Their modern counterparts look away from the hurt of the homeless as though they were not there. The lifeless lullaby of an anguished mother who must raise her infant child in inner-city squalor echoes the sound of David's plea, "Where are you Lord?" As in the psalms, so also here we find once again the wedding of music and misery.

The logic of how a loving God could allow children to die of AIDS, families to fall apart, and one's race or one's roots to form the basis of bigotry, remain mysteries that cry out for solution. Msgr. Oesterreicher's Hebraic answer to the mystery of Auschwitz may also signal some solutions elsewhere. The questions raised appear to be somewhat similar. Only a prophetic call for similar faith affords an answer.

Could it not be that in the hateful horrors of today, YHVH's spirit present in us is once again meant to be joined lovingly to the suffering of His people? Does not this suffering spirit of God in us impel us to return and seek the blessing of His presence without which we have no hope at all?

In his prophetic vision of the Holocaust, Msgr. Oesterreicher provides ancient insight into a modern mystery. He accomplishes, I believe, far more that. His call for a living act of faith gives promise that even in our hurting world, the hand of God is not absent.

THOMAS R. PETERSON, O.P.

BM 645 .H6 O37 1993

Oesterreicher, John M.,
 1904-

God at Auschwitz?

BM 645 .H6 O37 1993

Oesterreicher, John M.,
 1904-

God at Auschwitz?

DEMCO